Mermaids

a coloring book

Timothy R. Cook

Mermaids: a coloring book

Copyright © 2016 Timothy R. Cook

http://www.etsy.com/shop/TimCookArt

ISBN: 1533468958
ISBN-13: 978-1533468956

Printed by CreateSpace, an Amazon.com company.

Cover and interior illustrations by Timothy R. Cook.

Preface

This coloring book is a compilation of forty-eight drawings divided
into four sections that bring to life mermaids as envisioned by Tim Cook.
Inclusion of muscles in the tails gives structure to the mermaids' forms;
other important parts of their anatomy are dolphin-like flukes,
pelvic and vestigial dorsal fins which serve as identifying characteristics.

Acknowledgments & Inspiration

Alphonse Mucha's art is the primary source of inspiration
for the technical style and fashion design of these drawings,
and the graceful elegance and inherent strength of ballet
with its fluid lines of form and motion are the most
important stylistic influence. Underwater photographers like
Howard Schatz, Zena Holloway, Vitaly Sokol, Todd Essick,
Shawn Heinricks, and others have all been instrumental
in the development of the vision surrounding these mermaids.

Part I

the zodiac

The twelve zodiacal constellations
are portrayed here as mermaids
and their kin, their forms following
the arrangements of stars while
alluding to traditional representations
of each sign.

Colors by _____

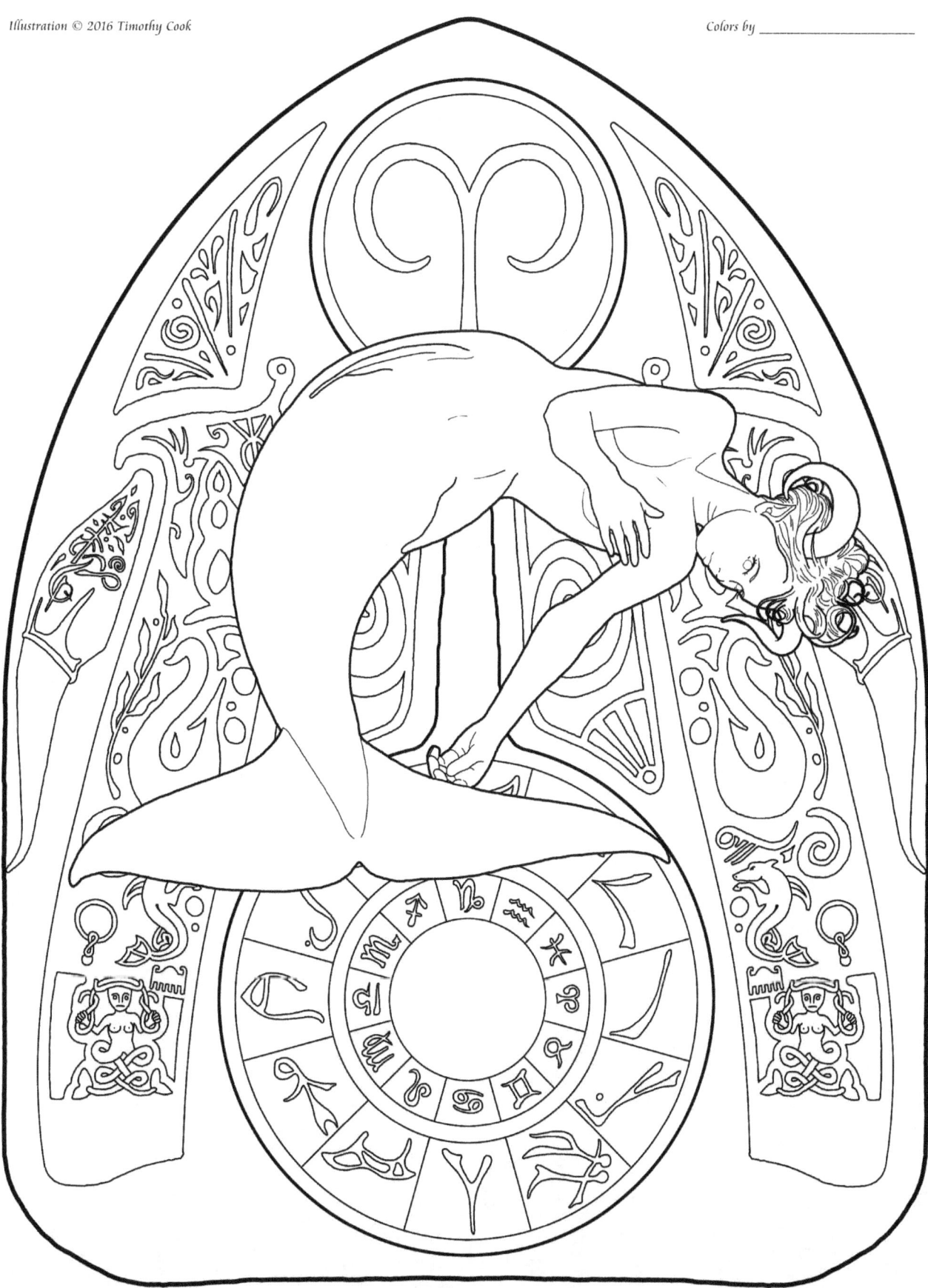

Colors by _____

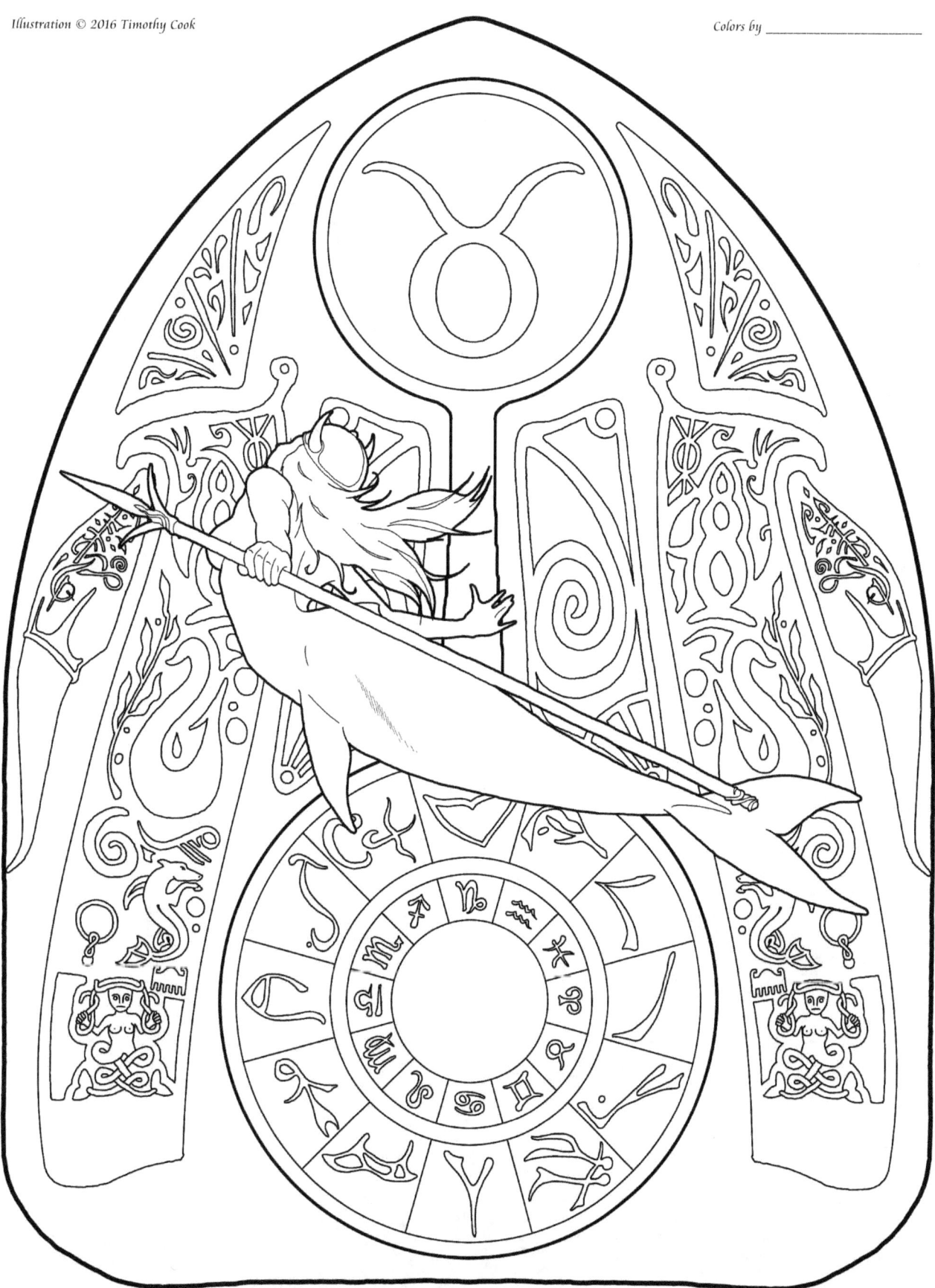

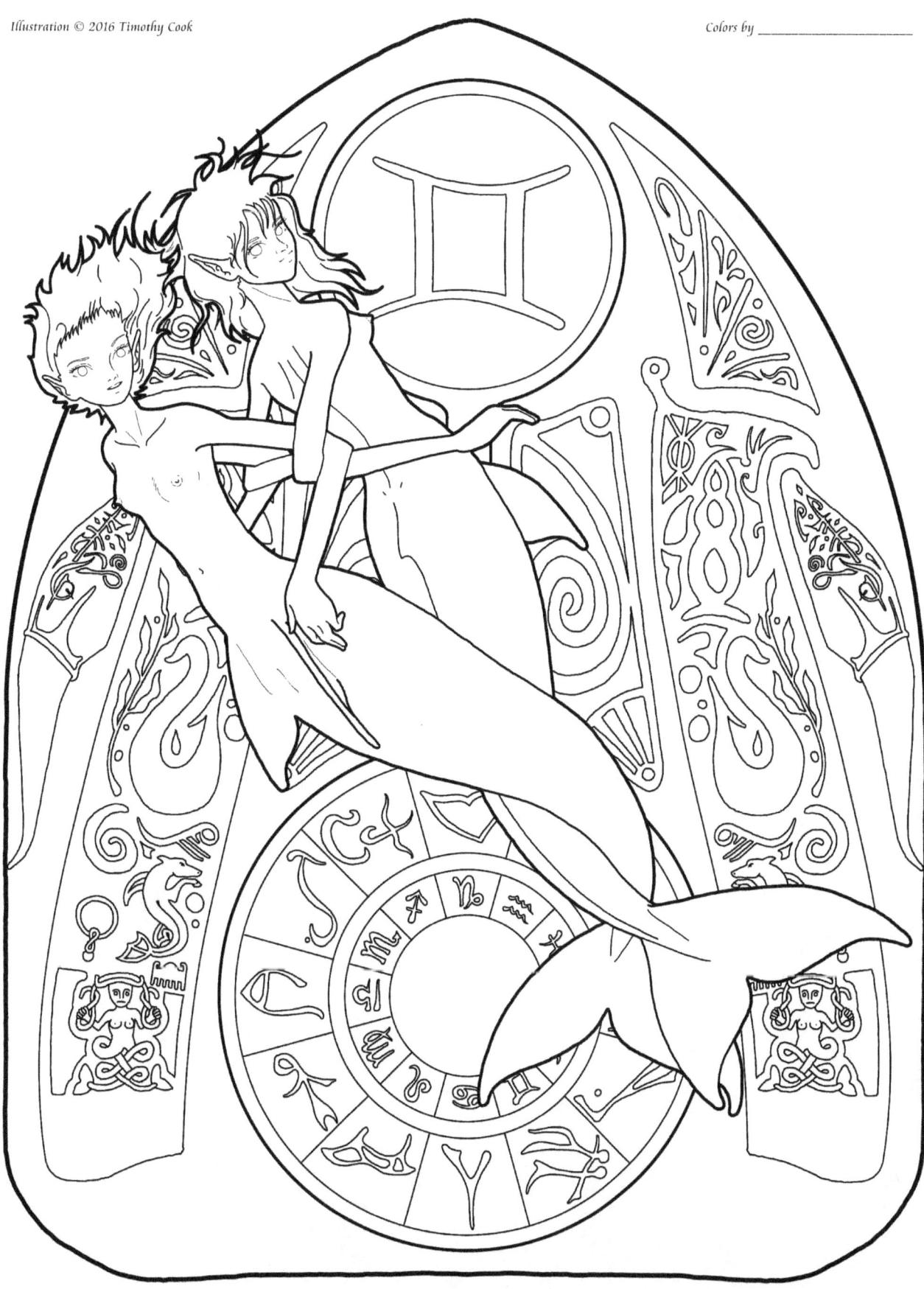

Colors by _____

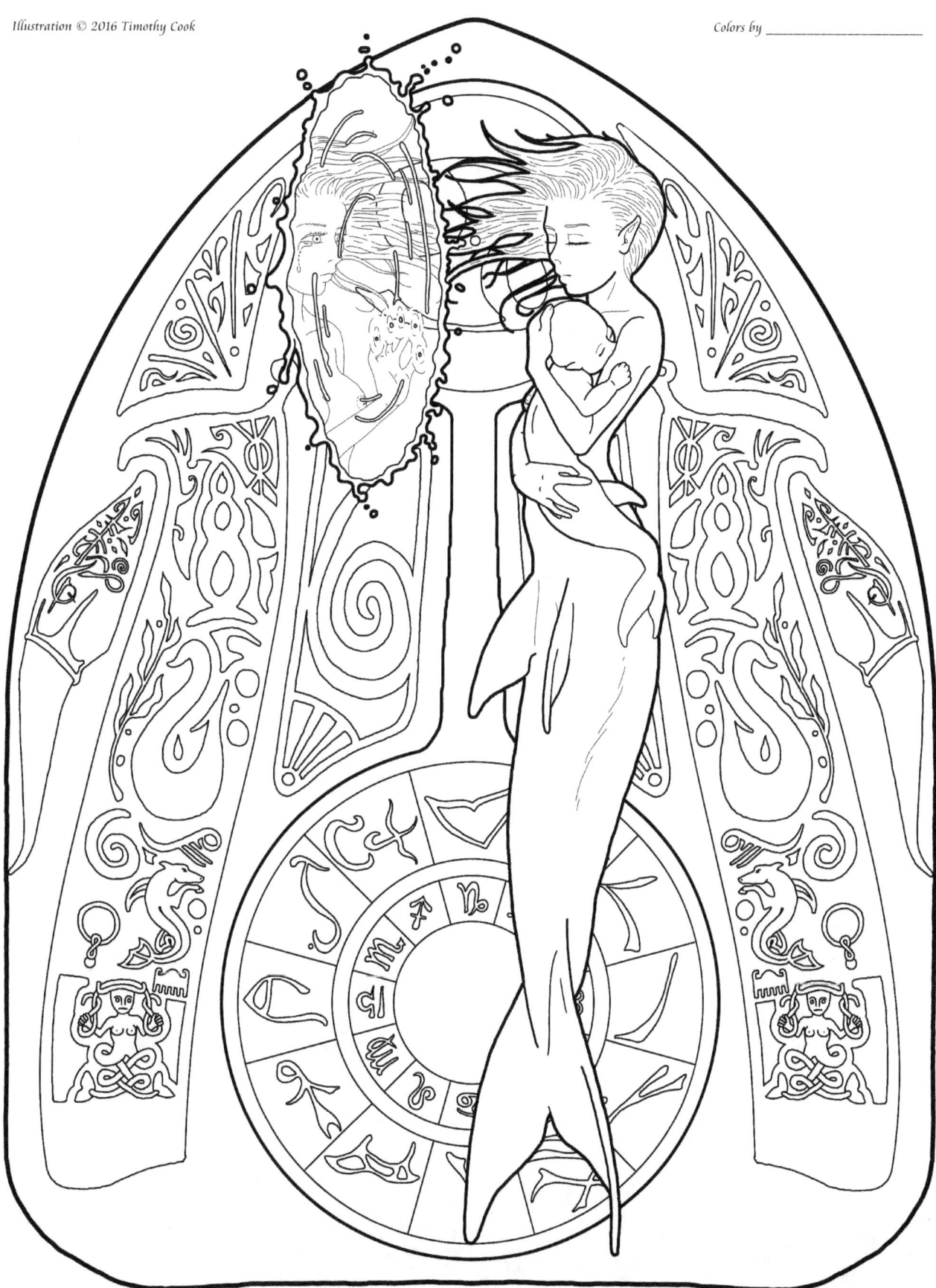

Colors by _____

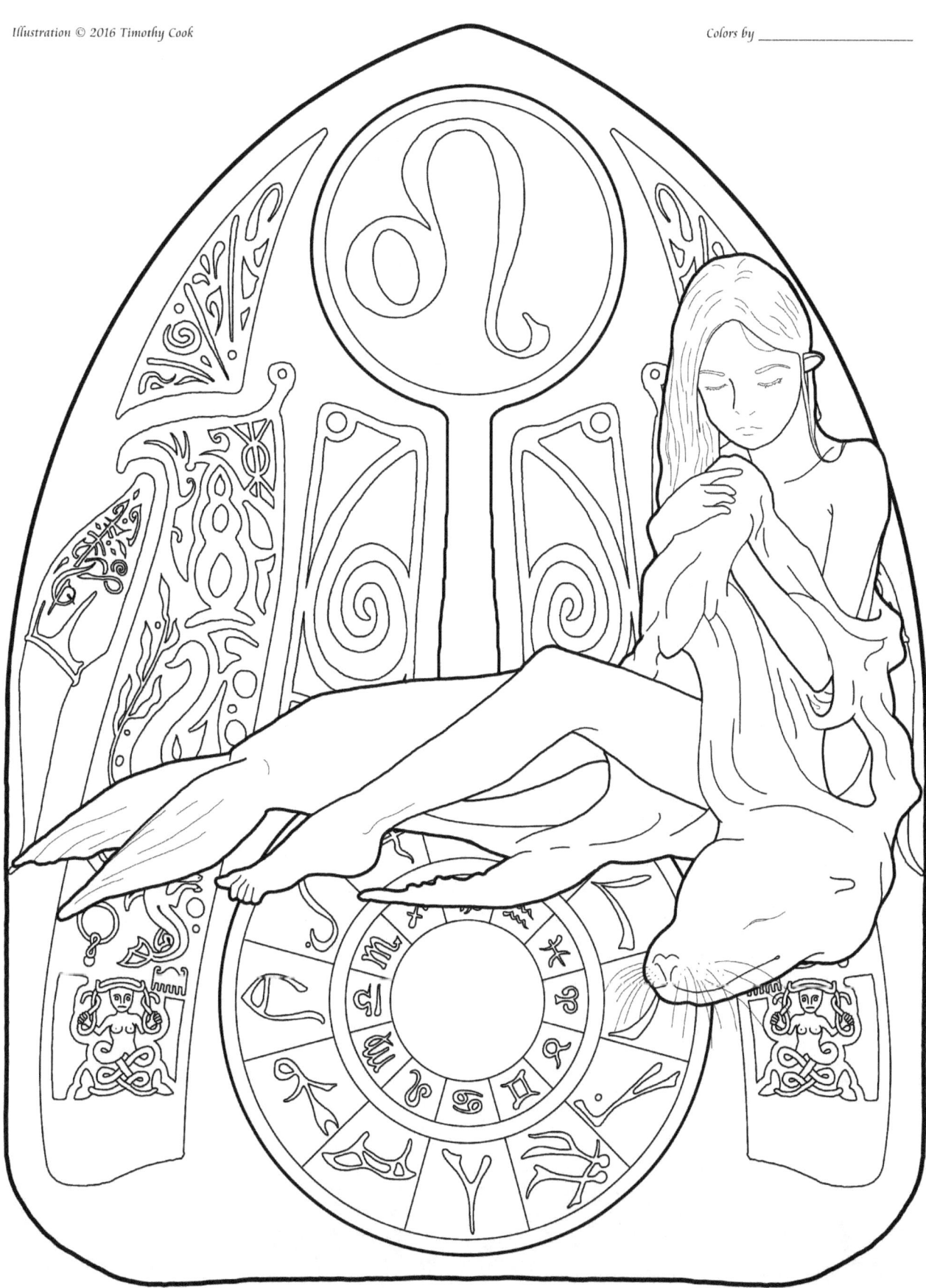

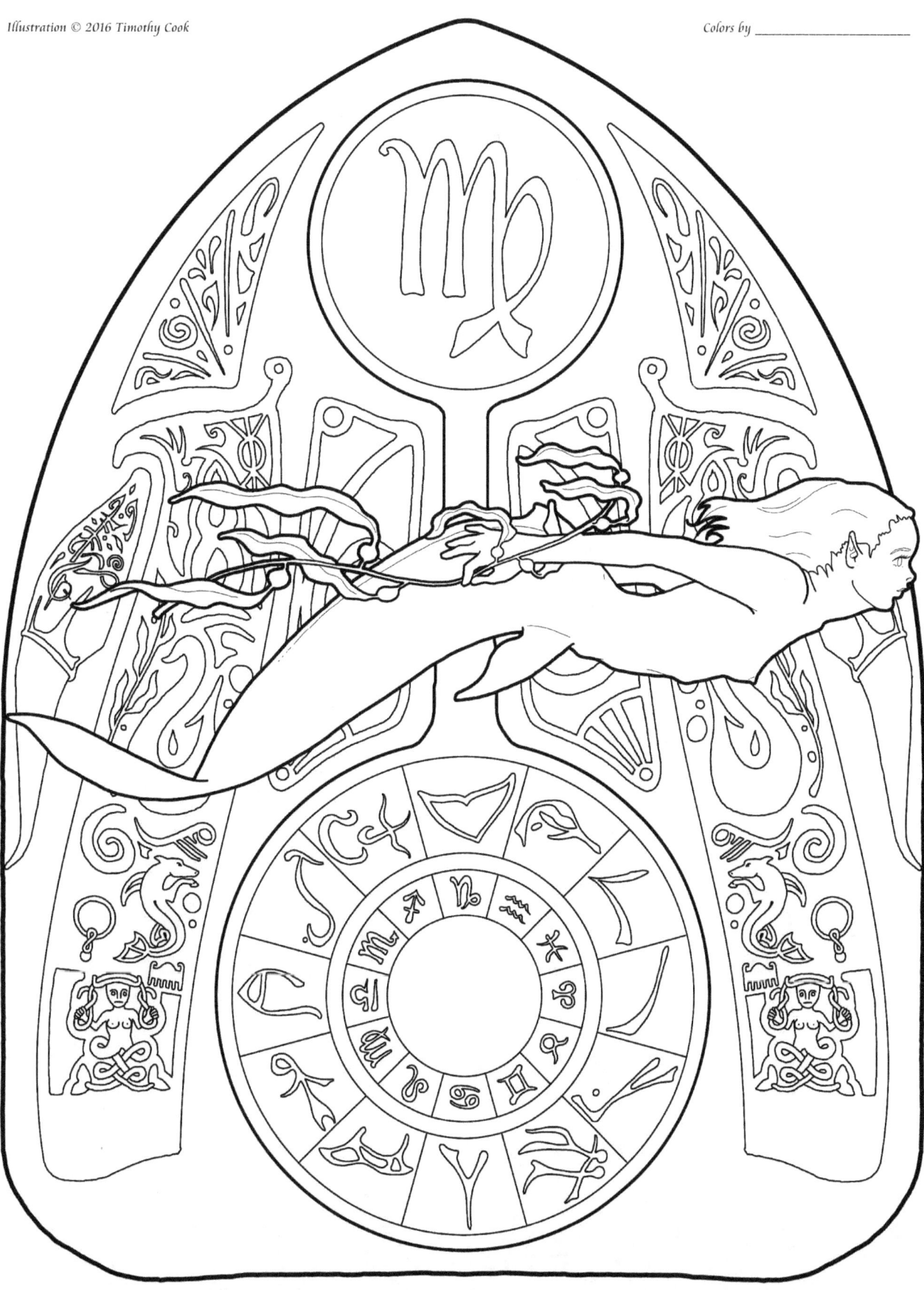

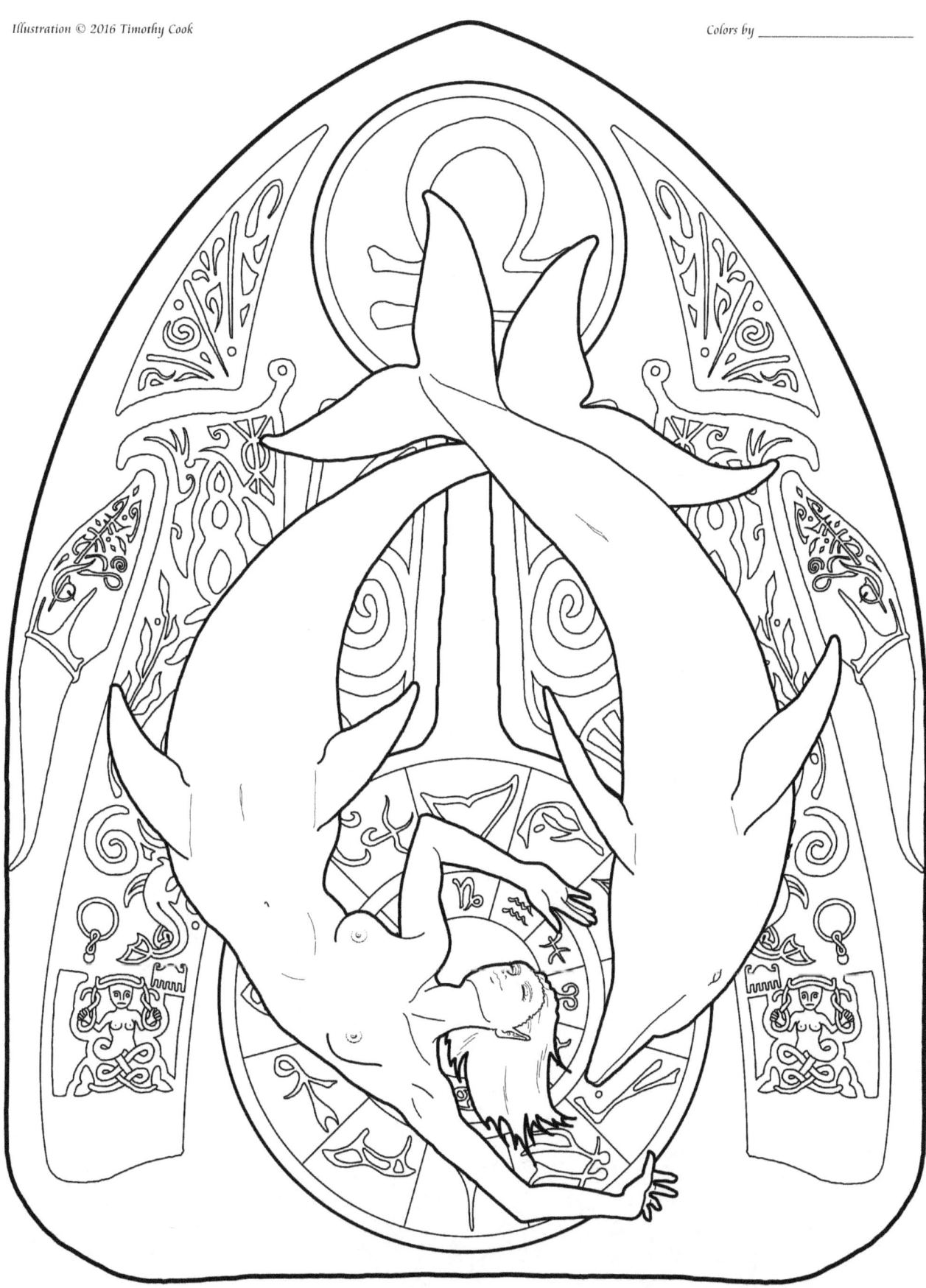

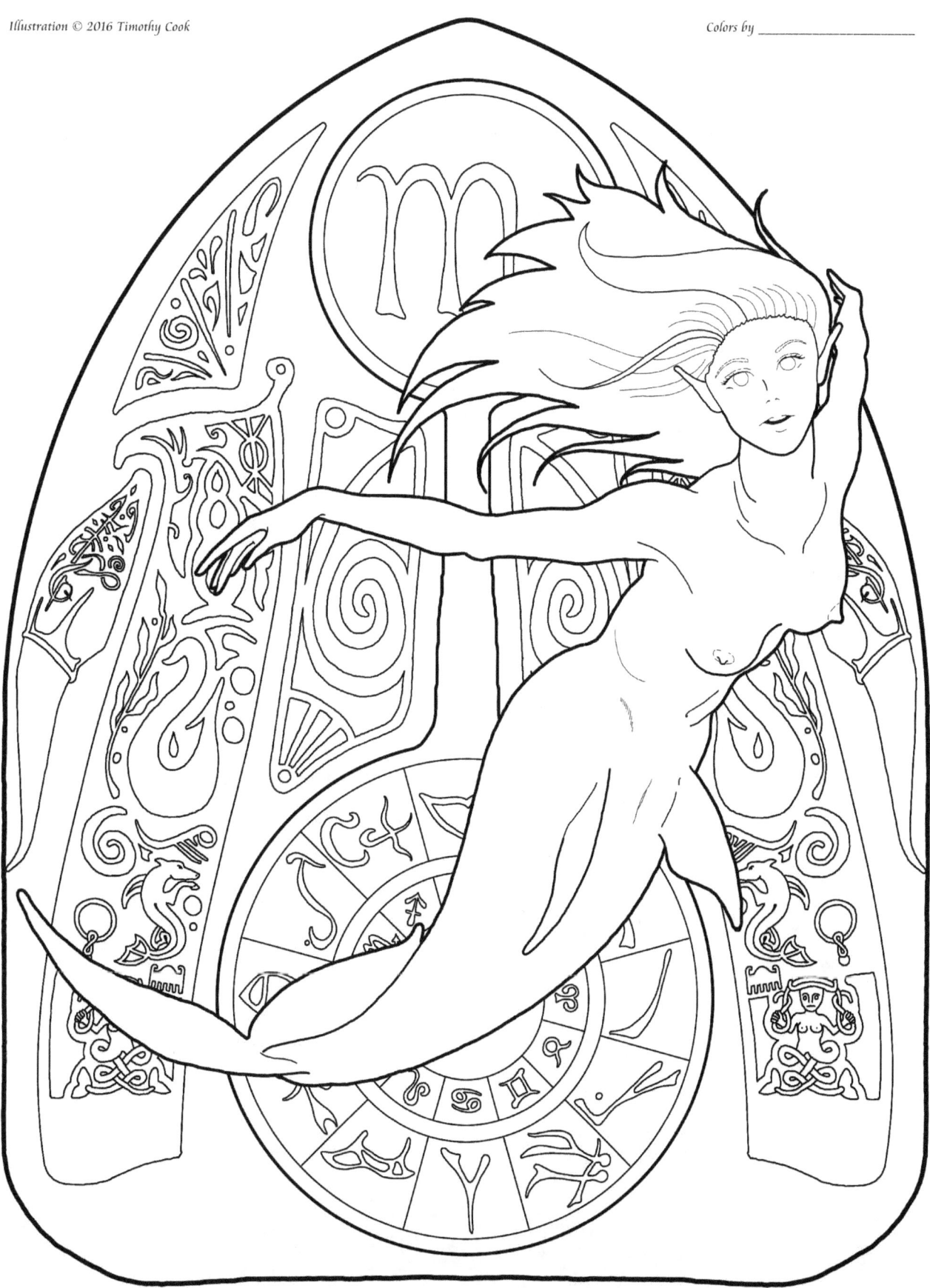

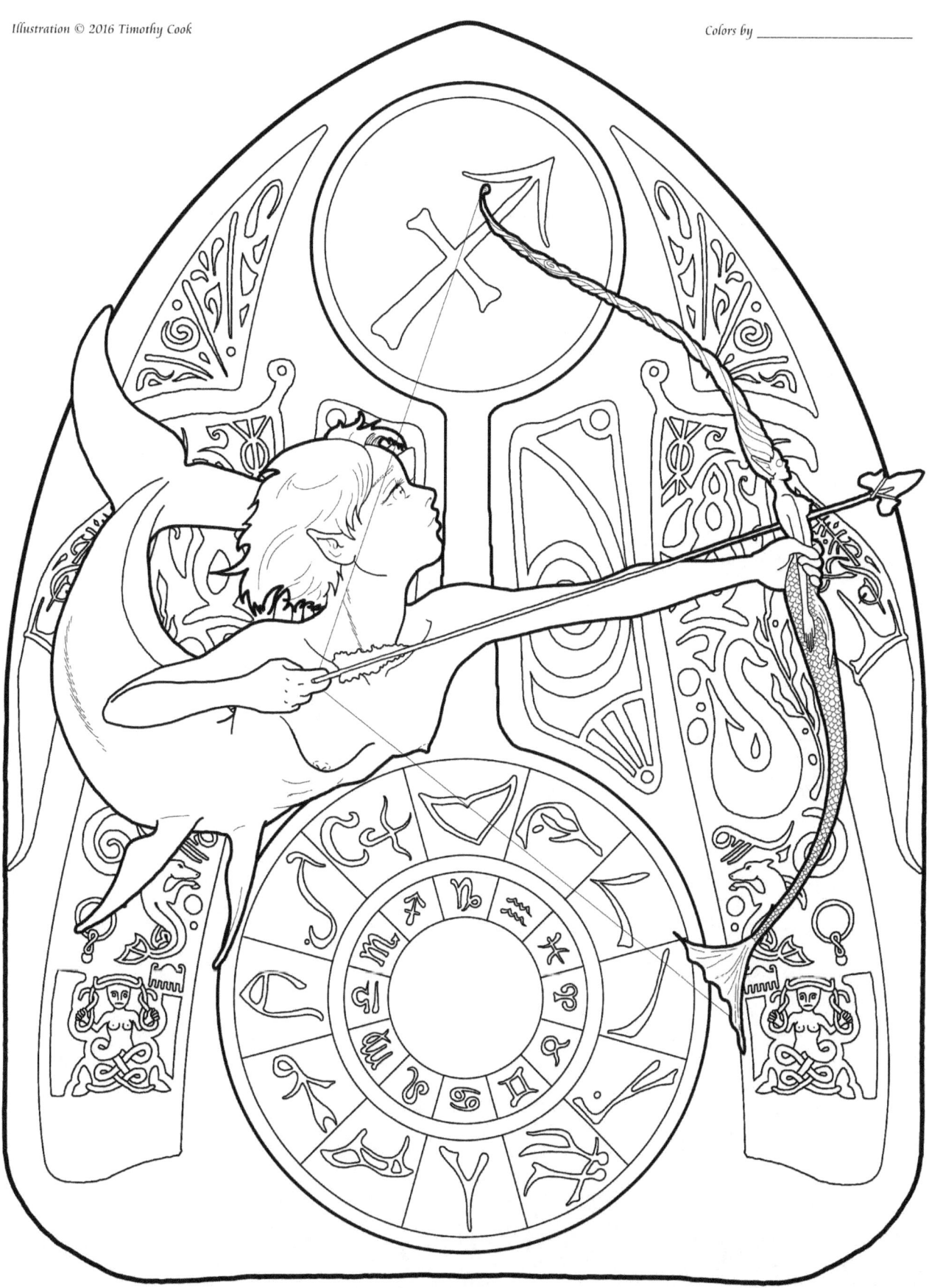

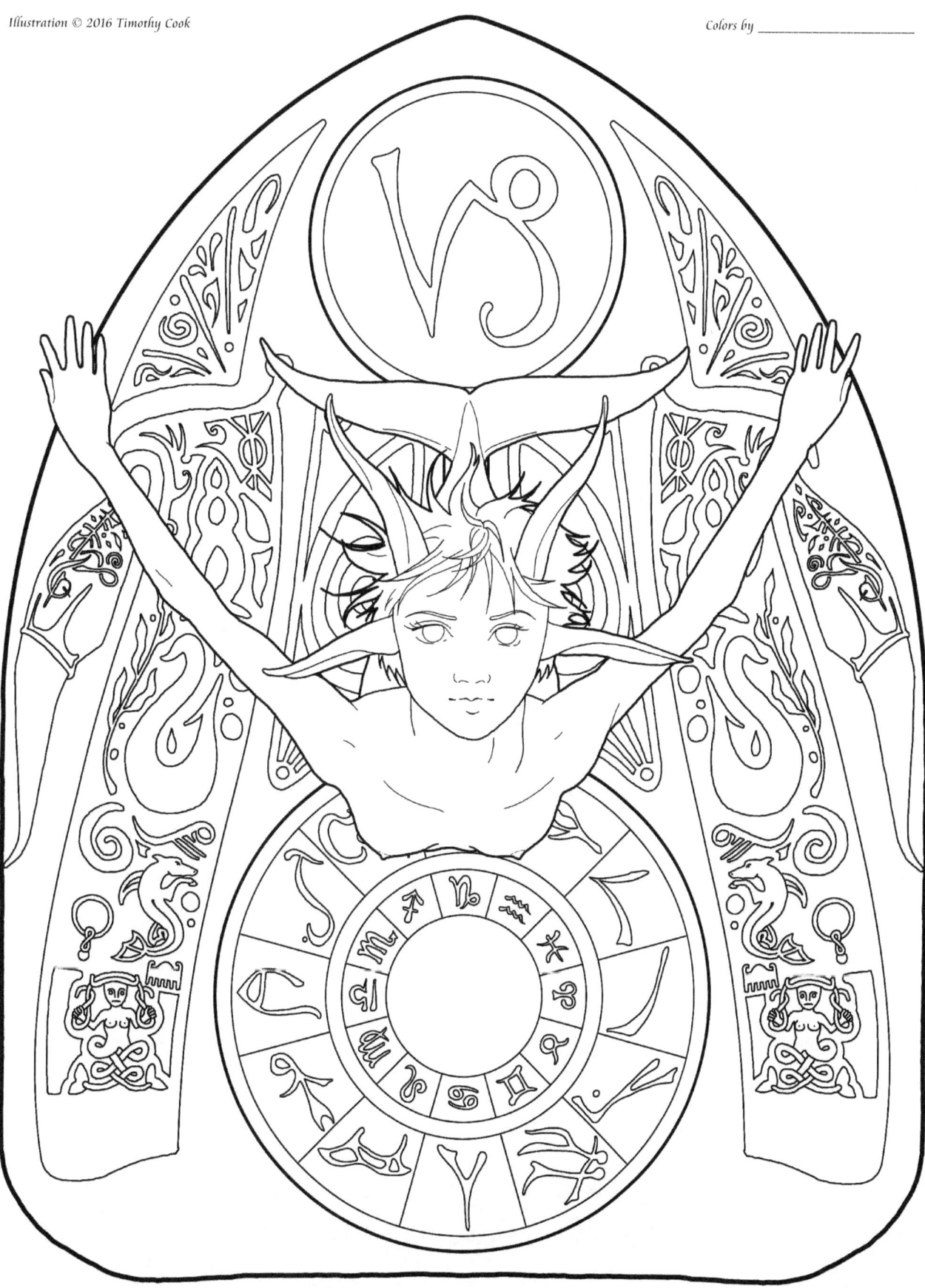

Colors by _____

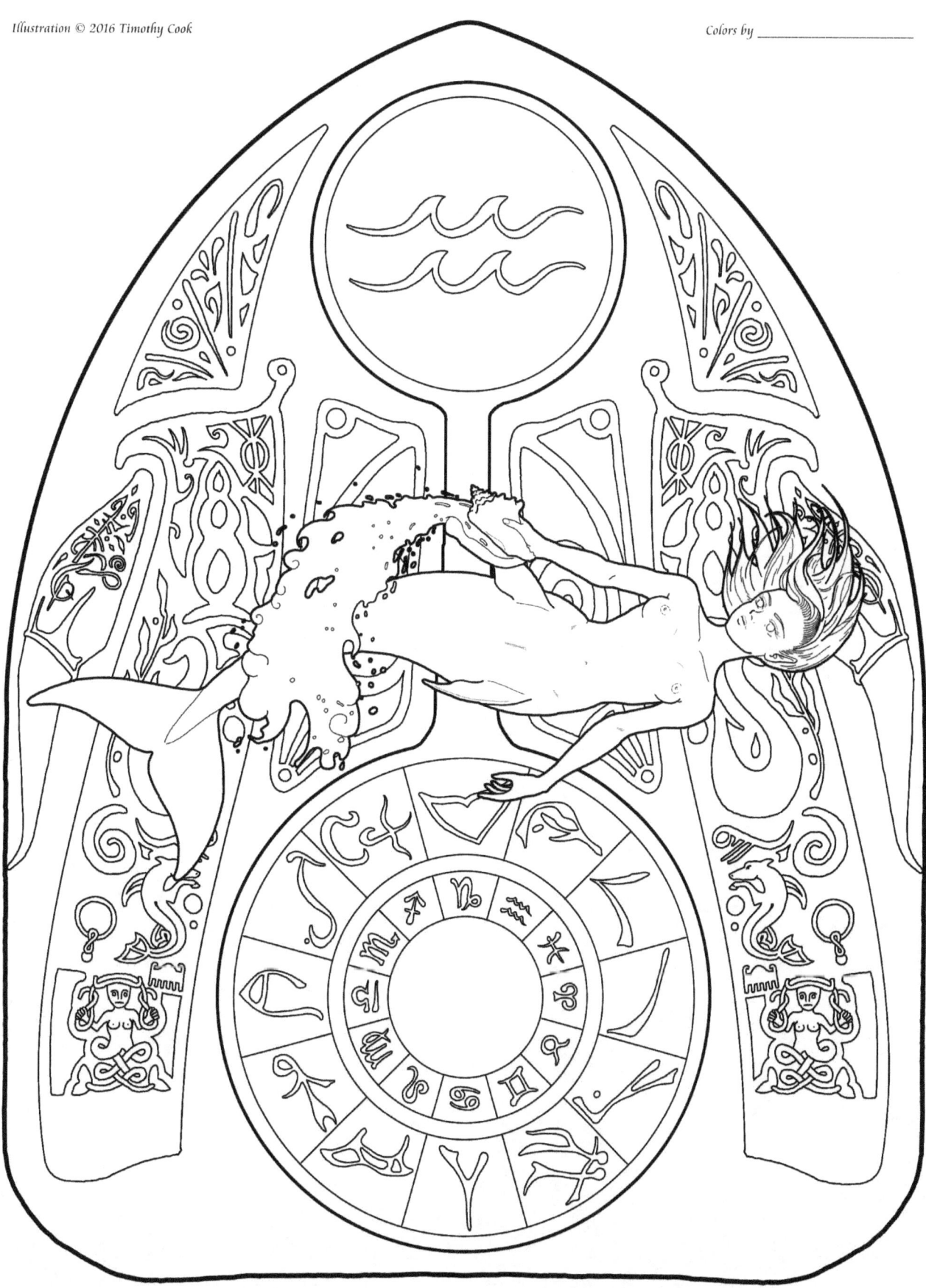

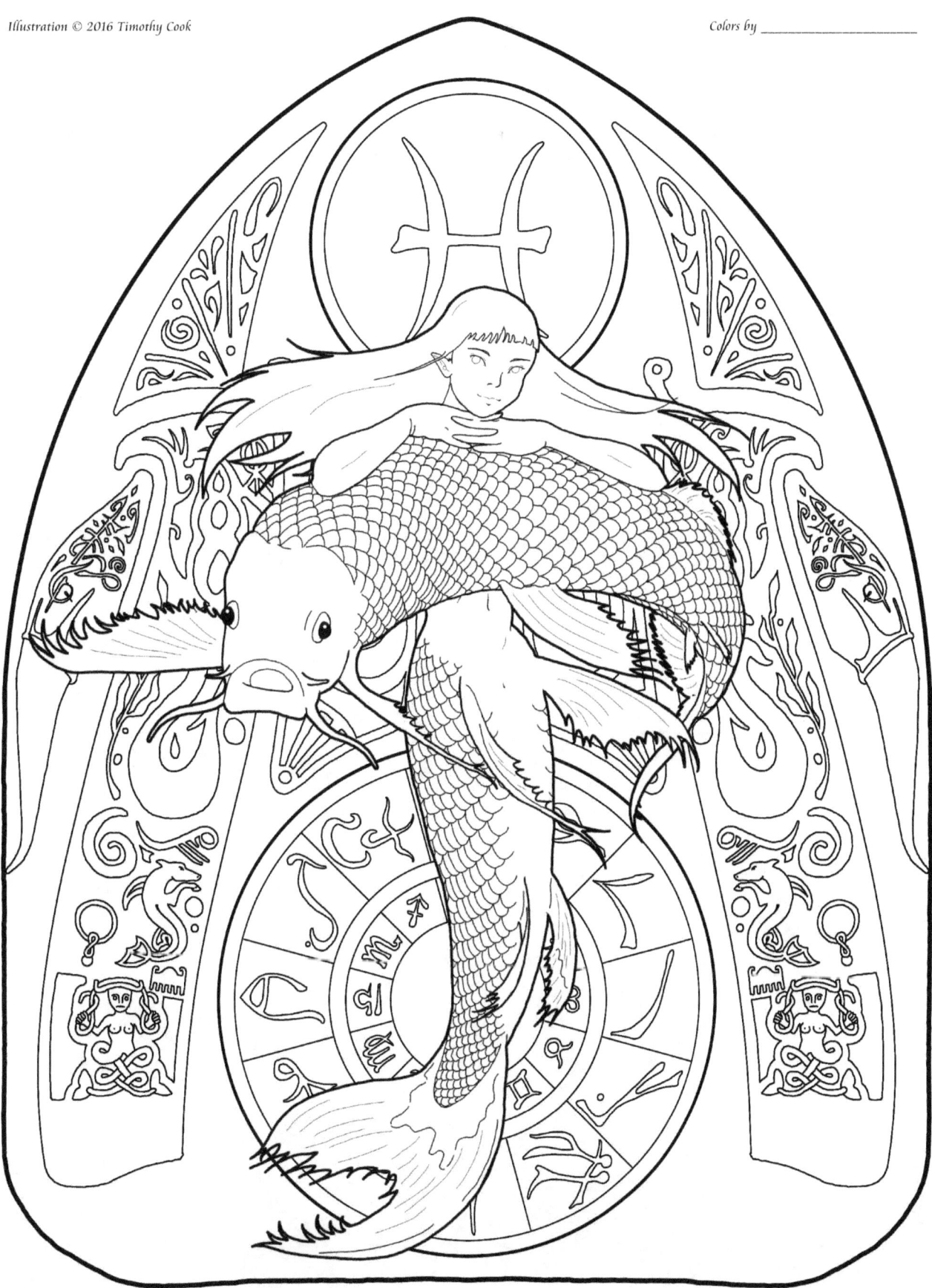

Part II

unity

Individually, mermaids share the wild freedom and tempestuous passion of the sea. Their detachment from the mundane world, however, is burdened by a profound loneliness.

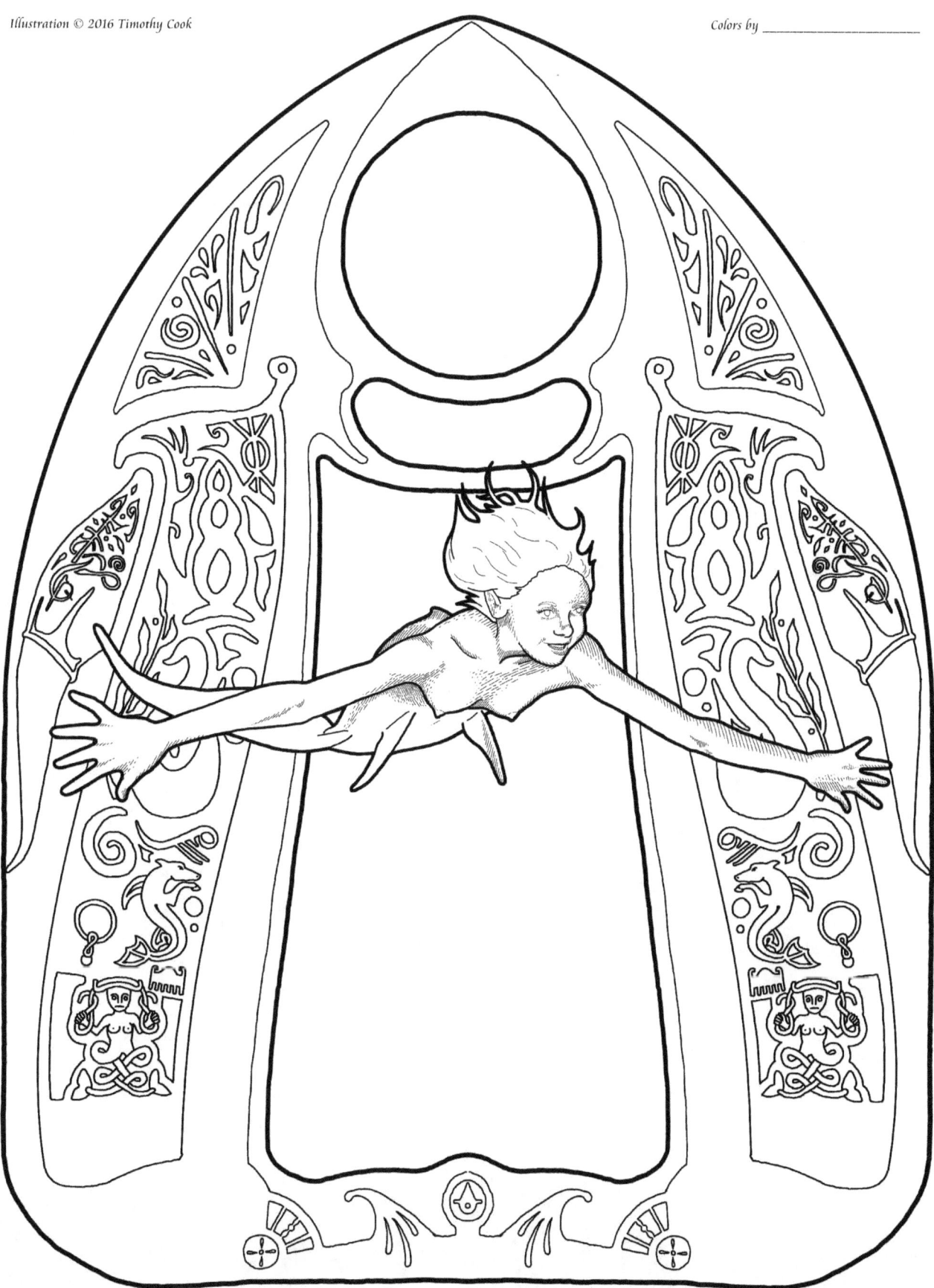

Colors by _____

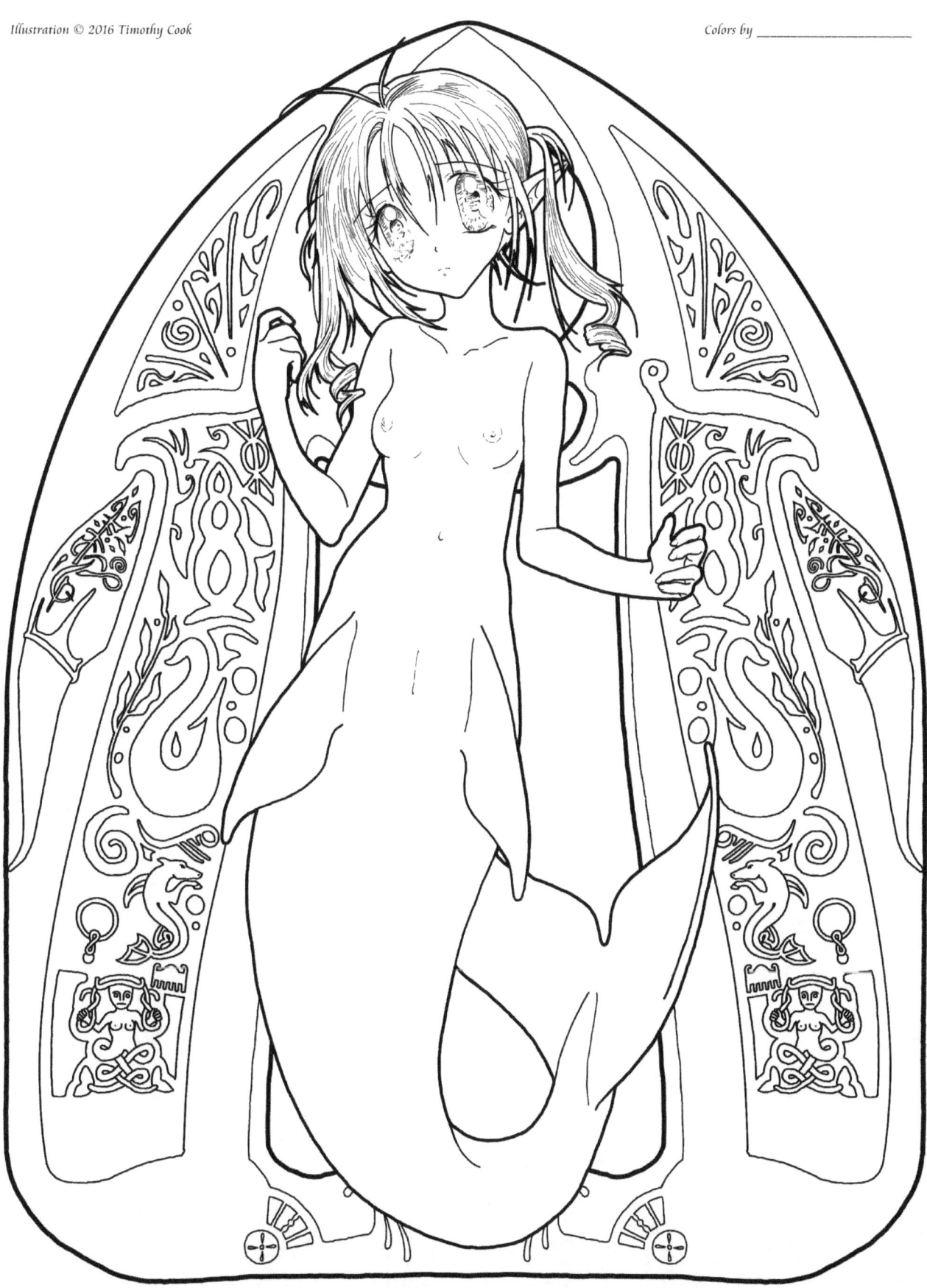

Colors by _____

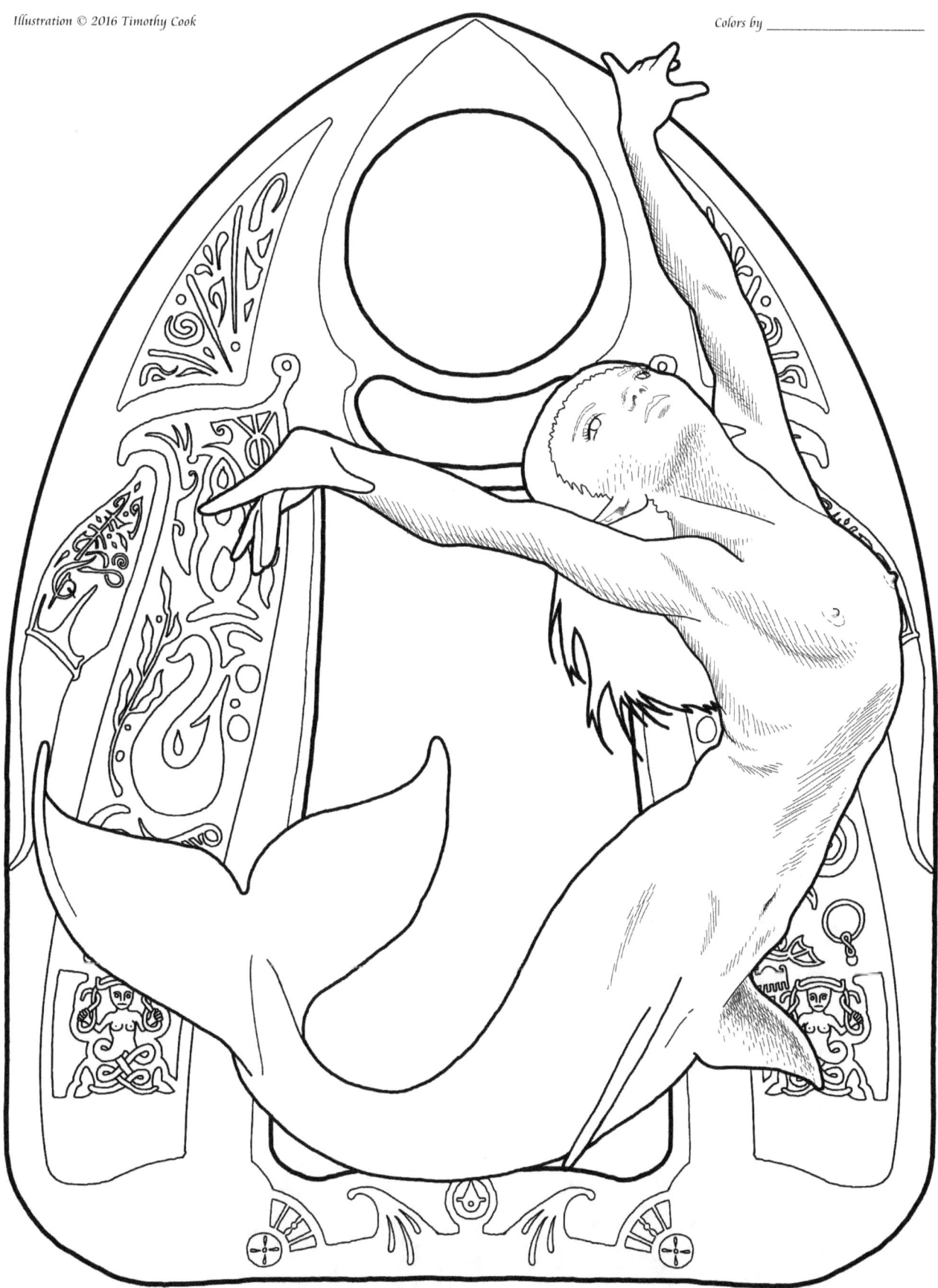

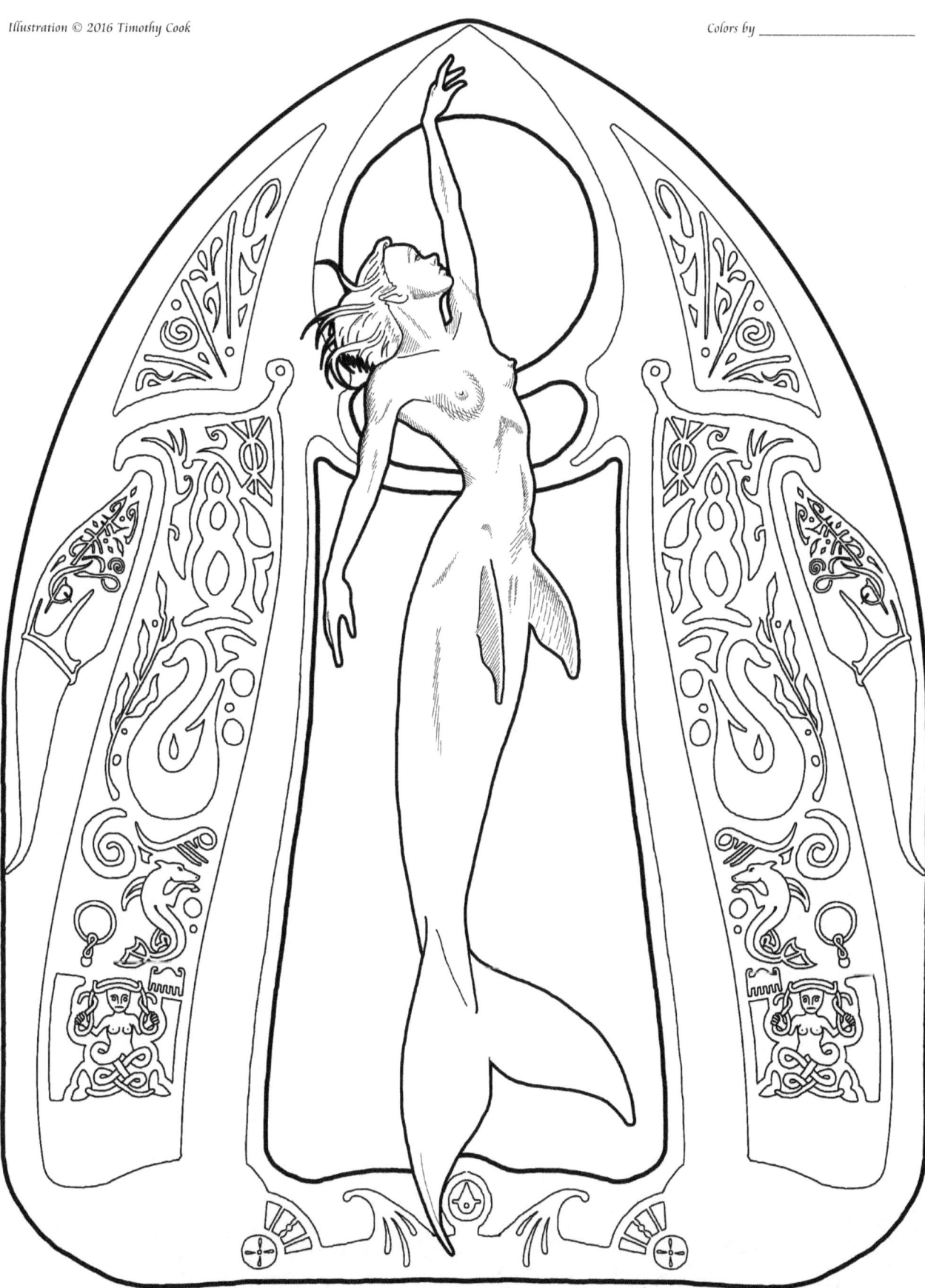

Colors by _____

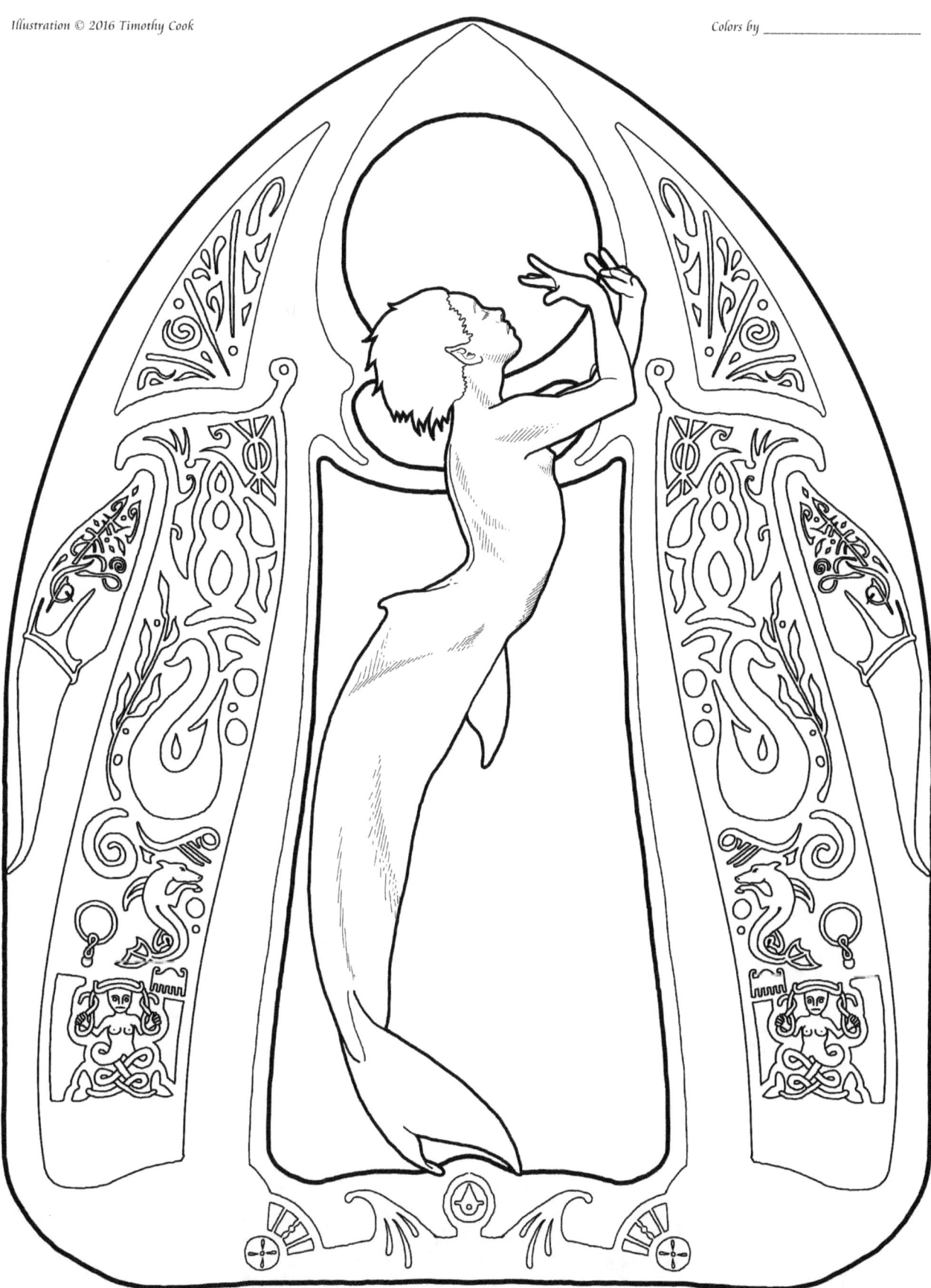

Colors by _____

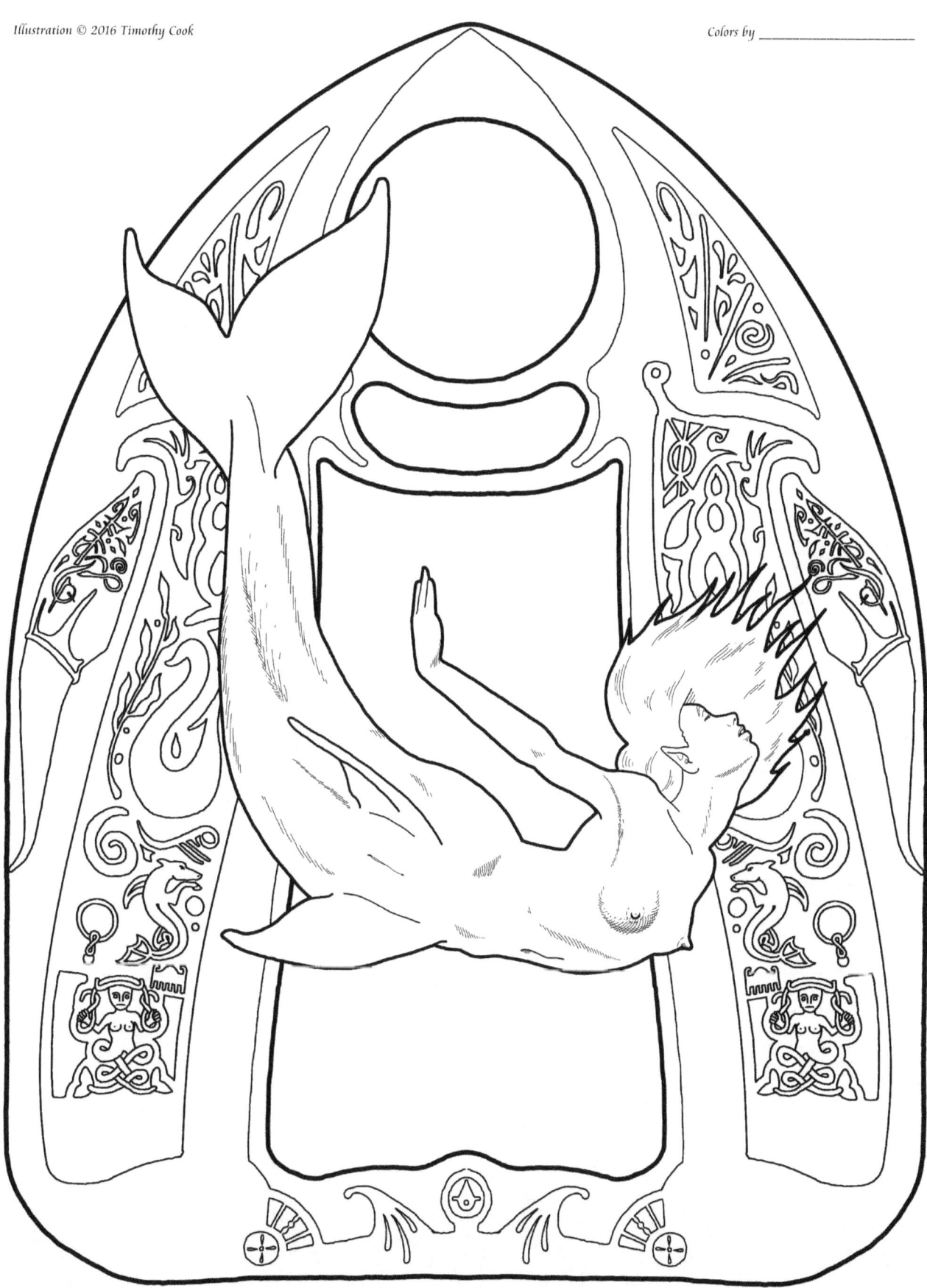

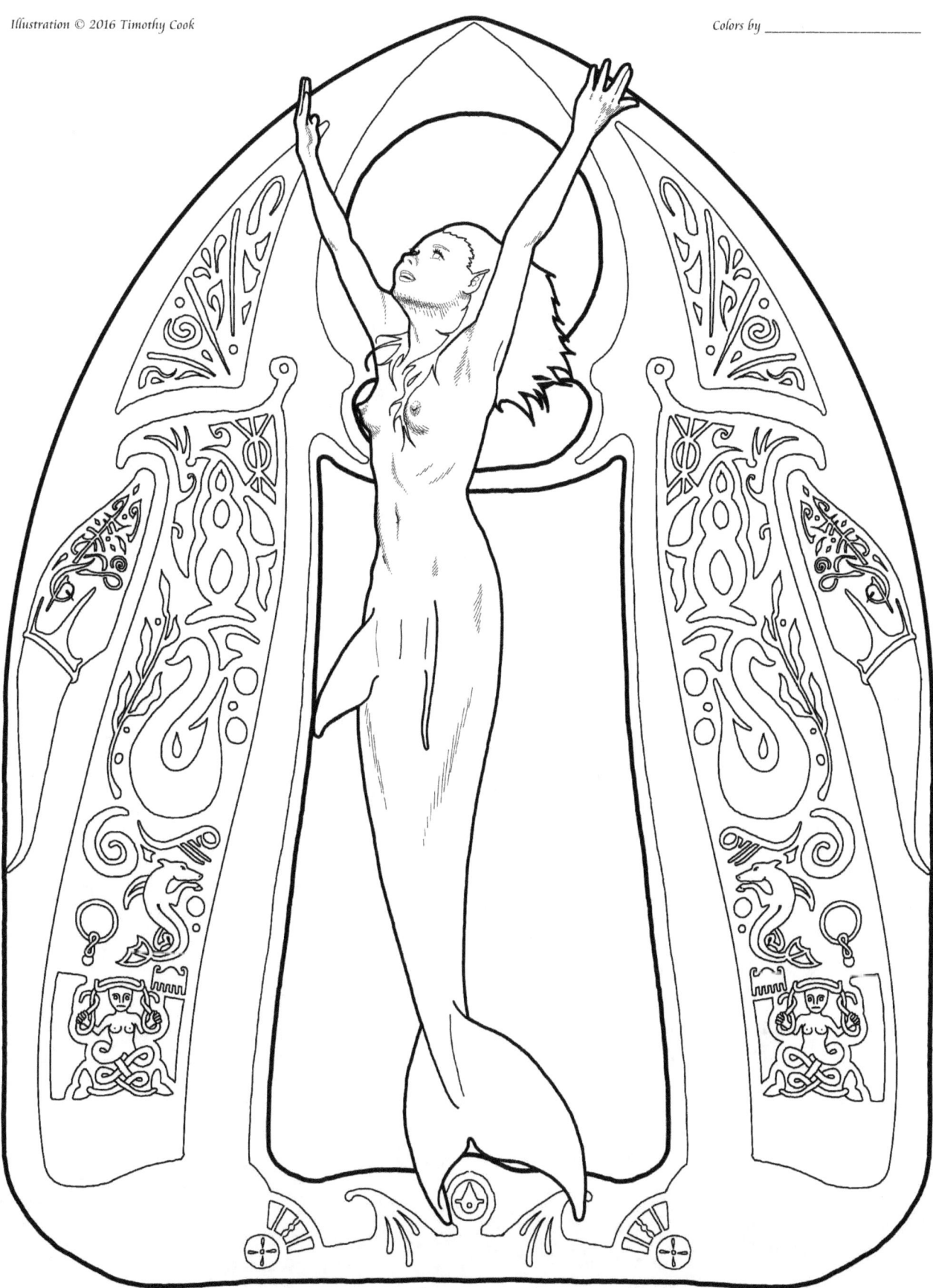

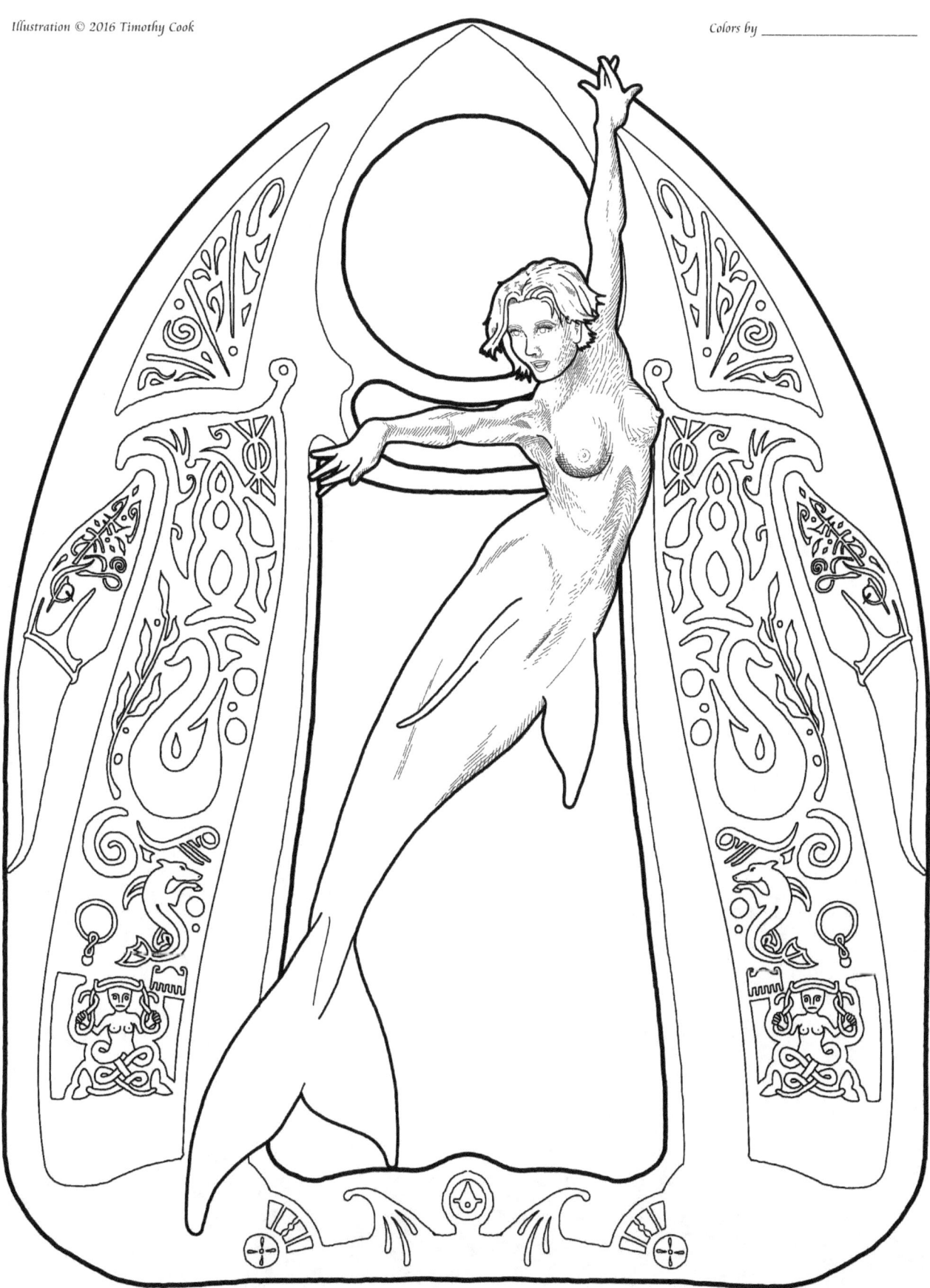

Colors by _____

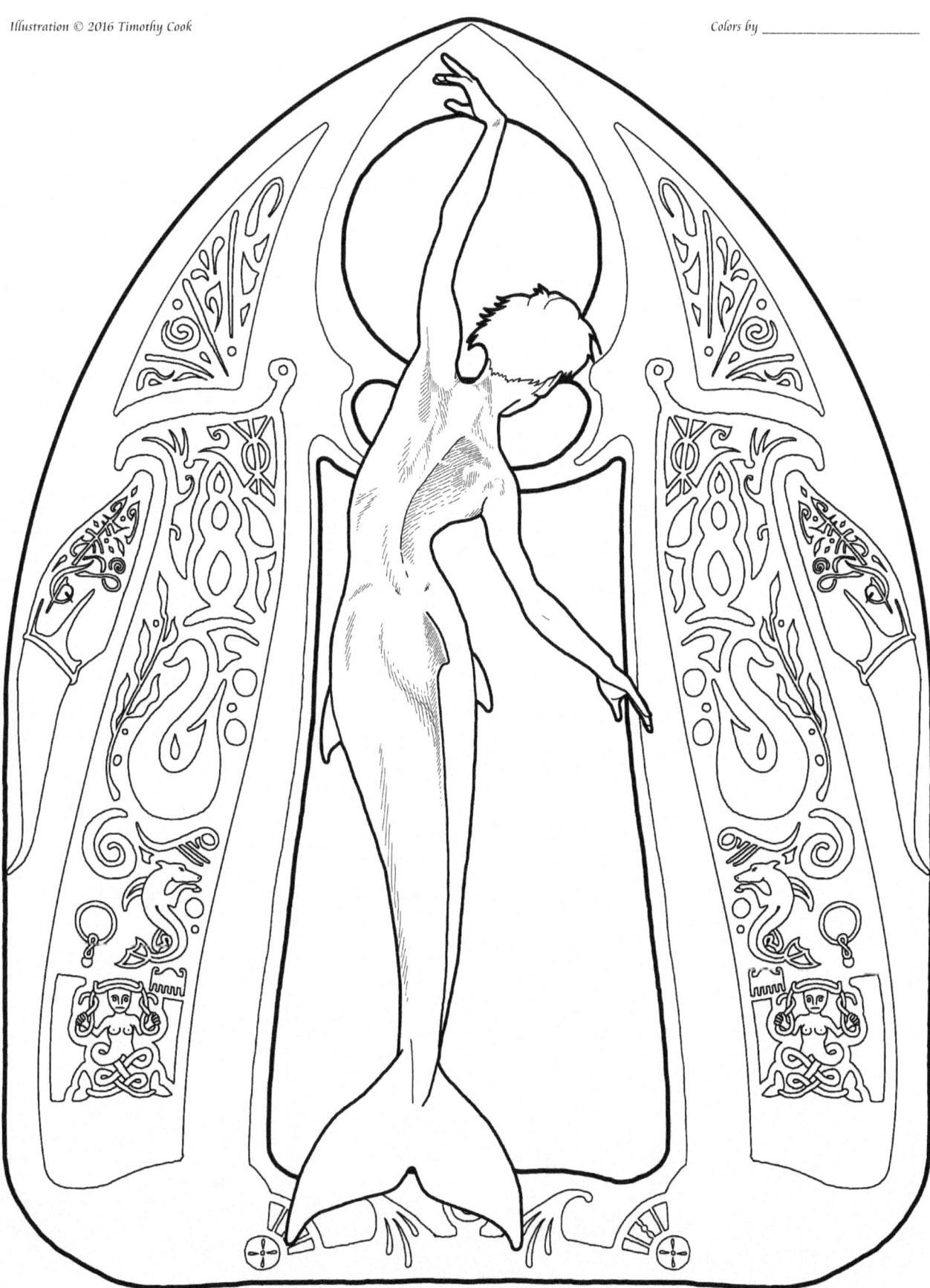

Colors by _____

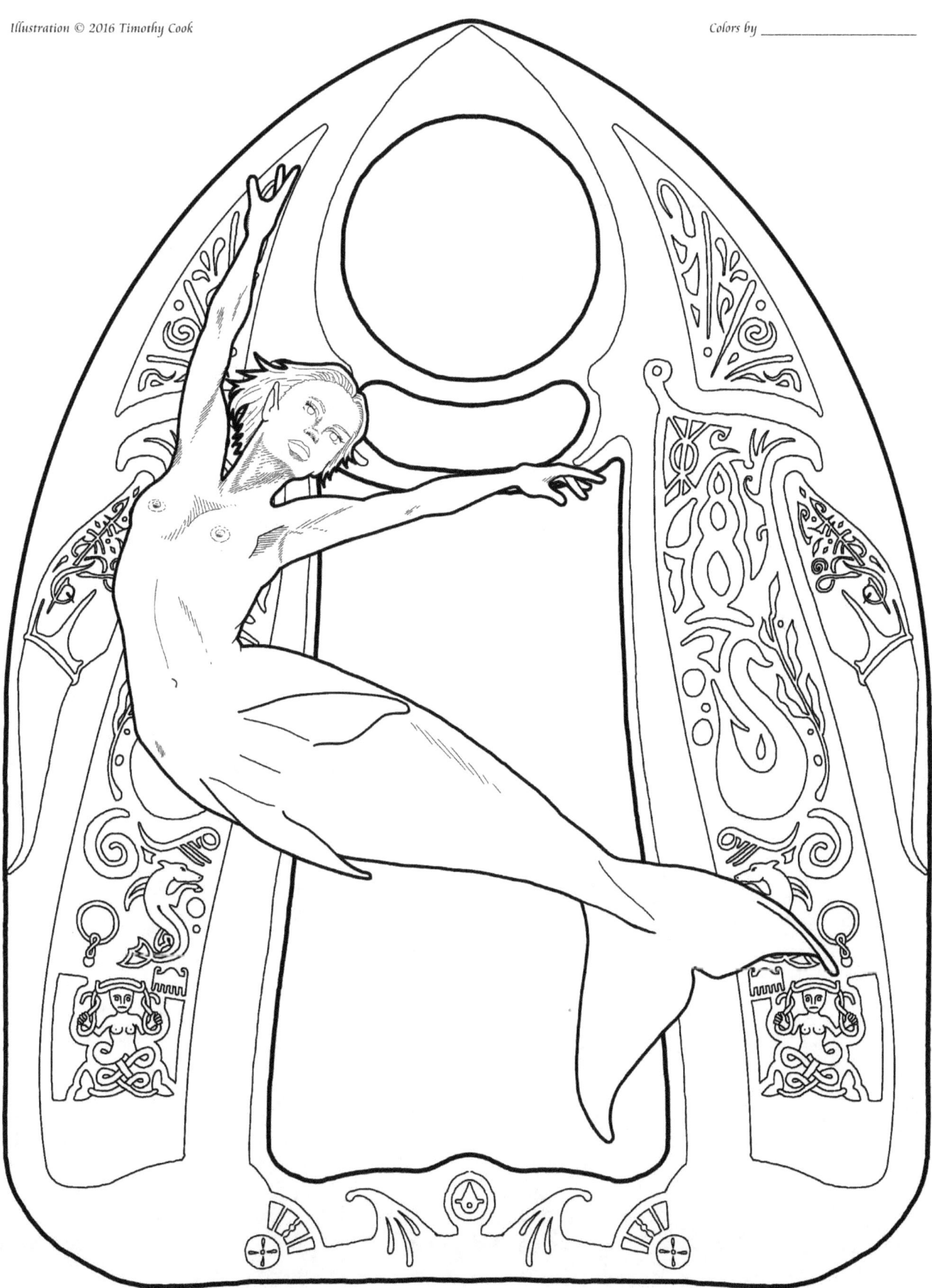

Colors by _____

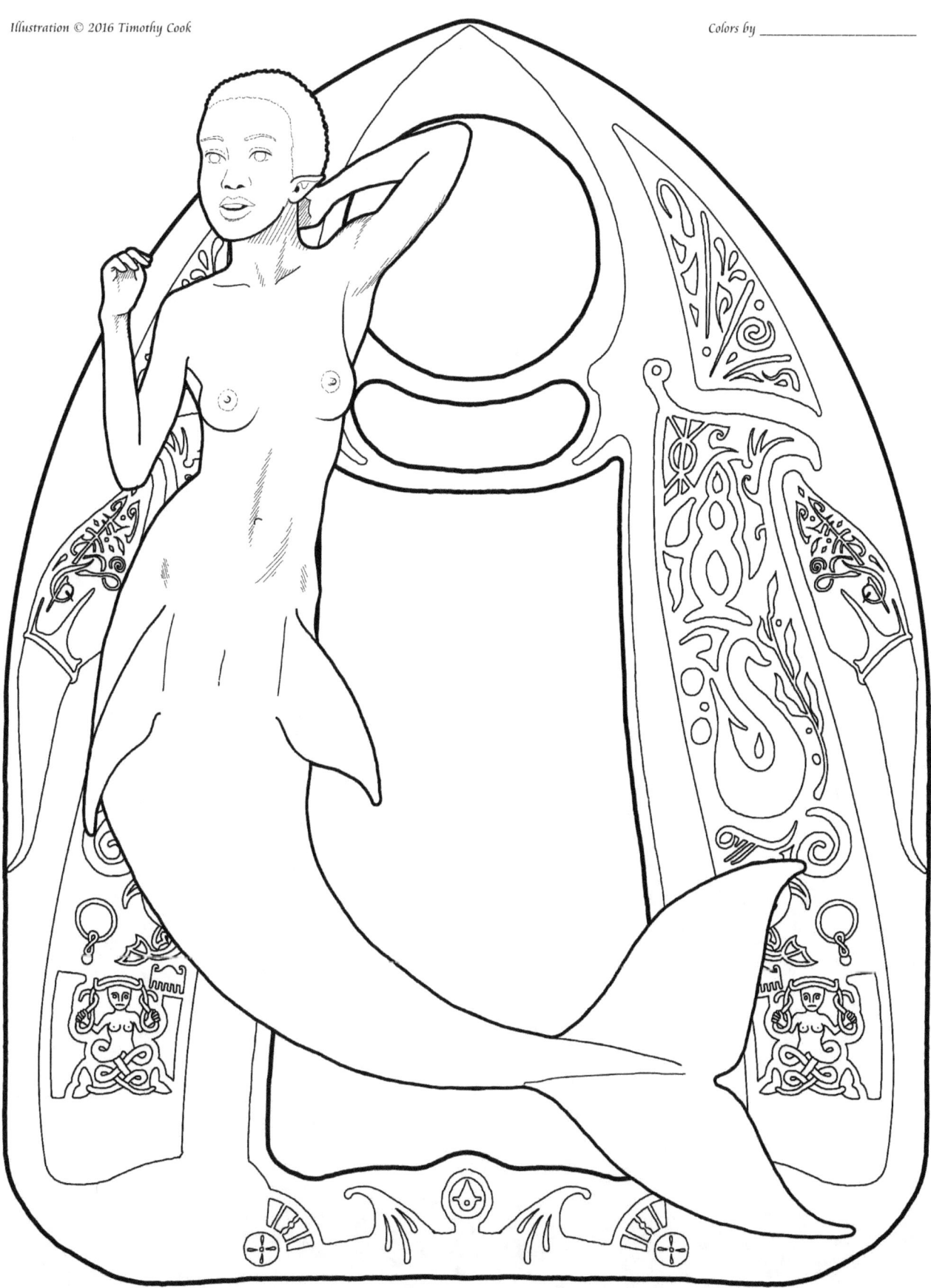

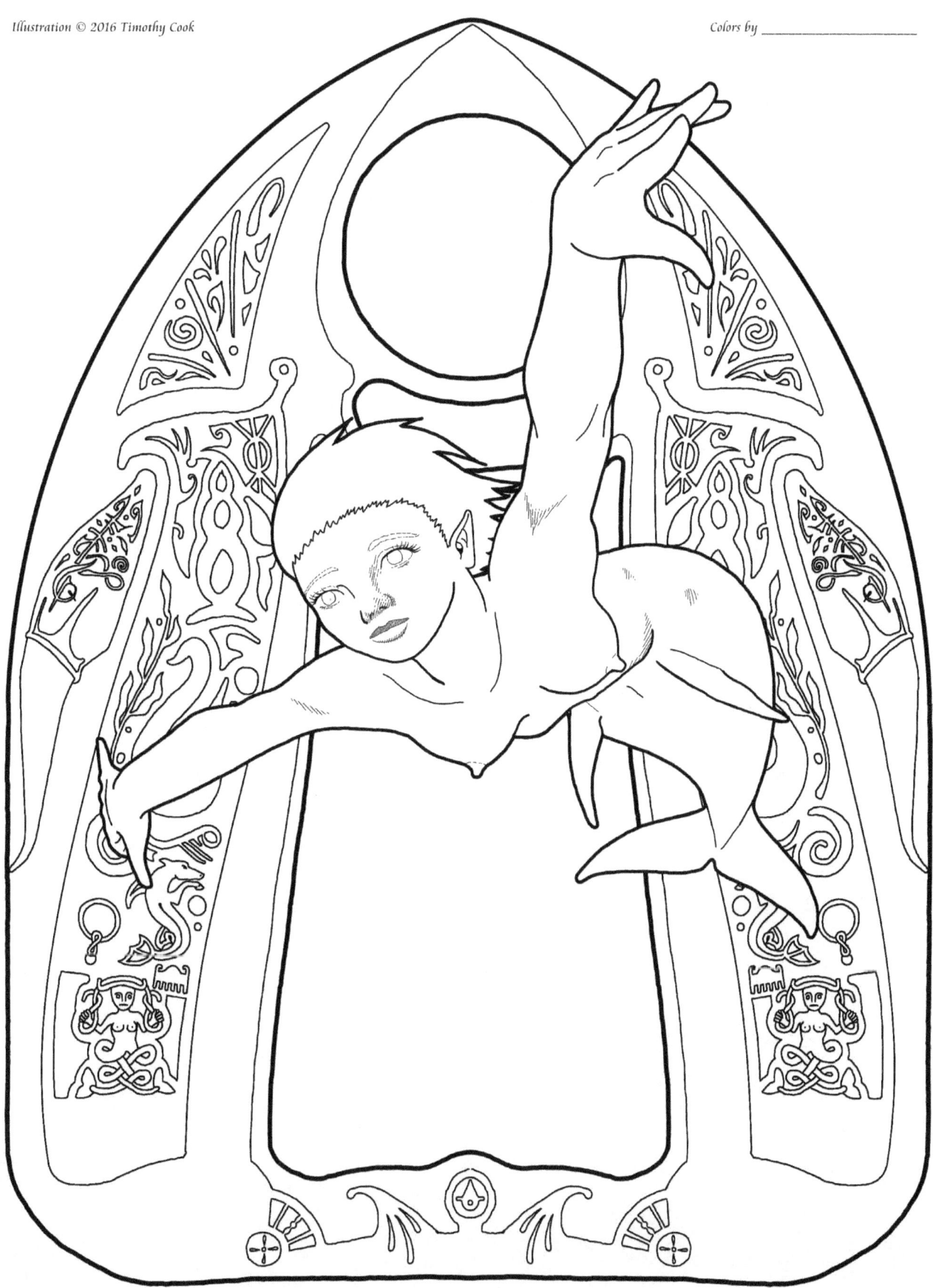

Part III

pas de deux

Twinned spirits shine brighter
than the mere sum of both;
harmony and communion
between two souls becomes a
beacon to uplift those
hearts it illuminates.

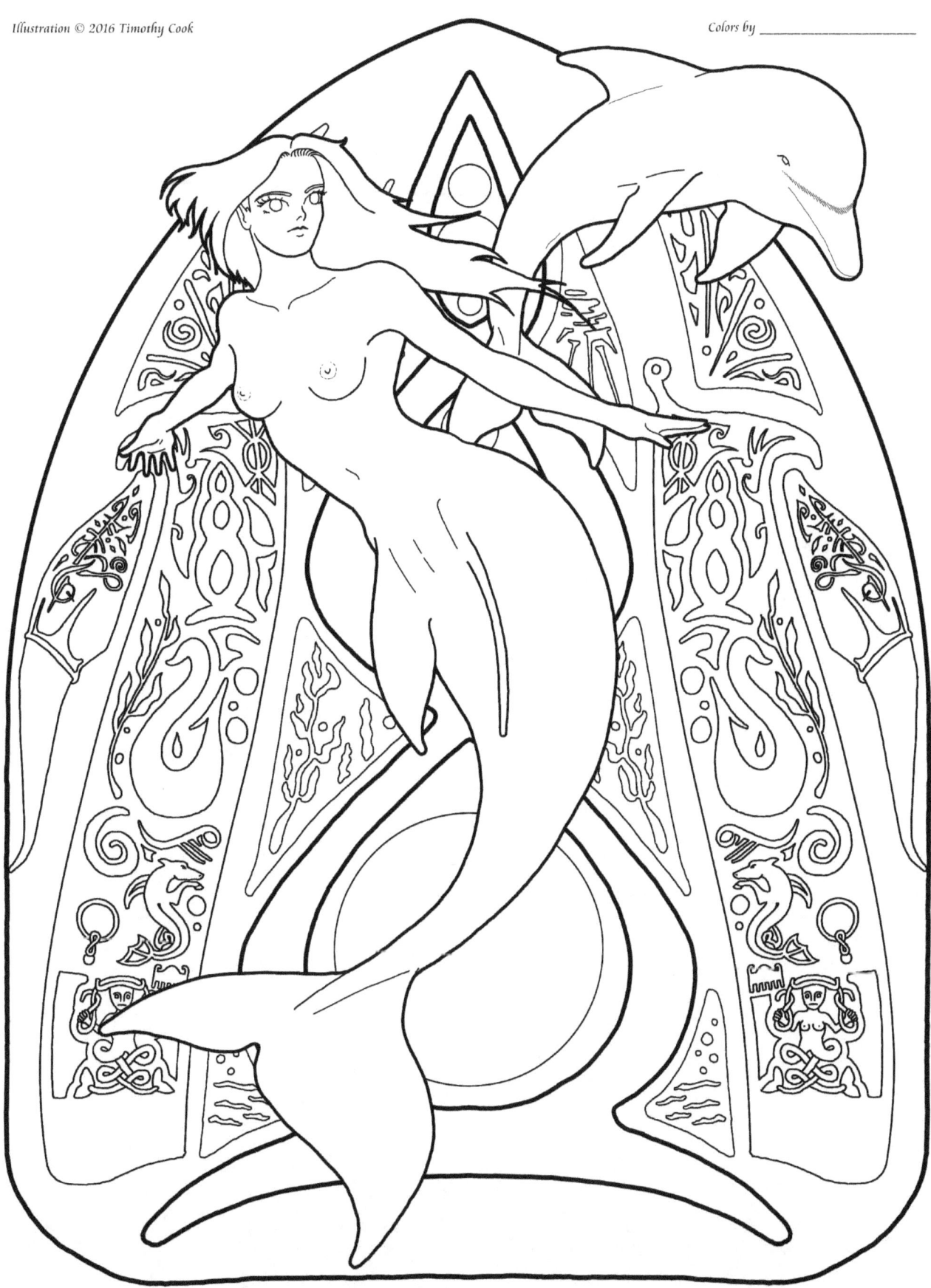

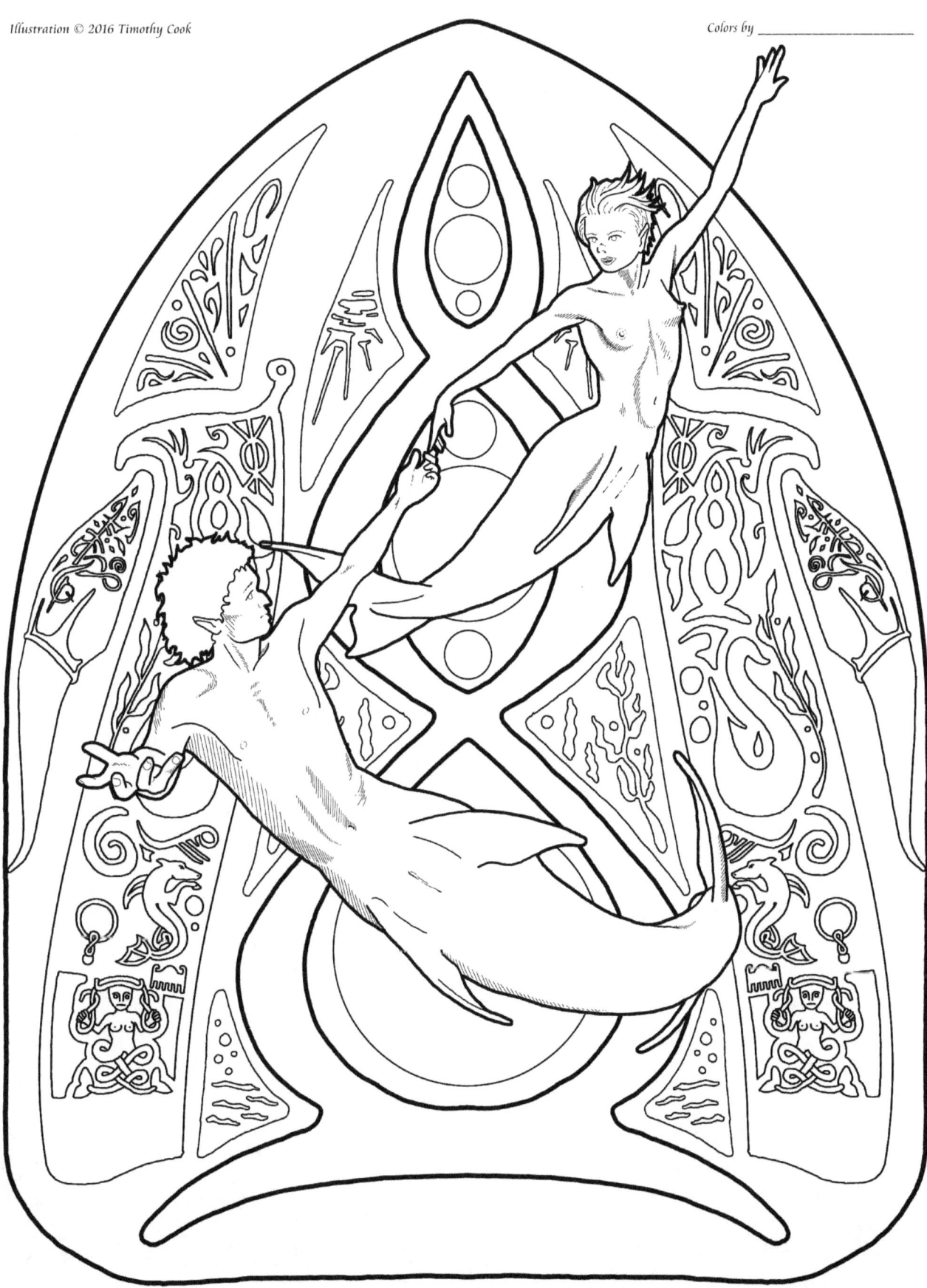

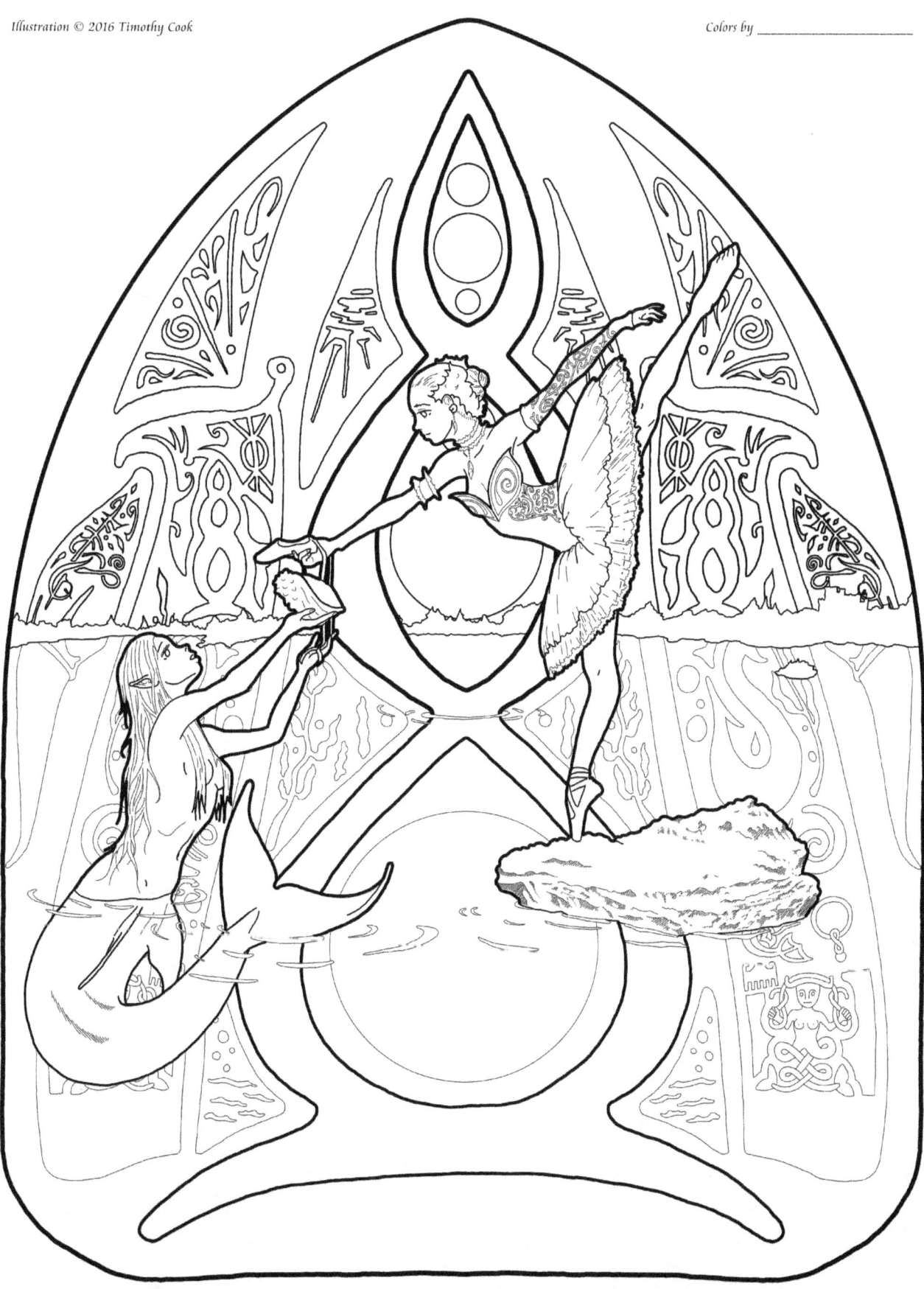

Colors by _____

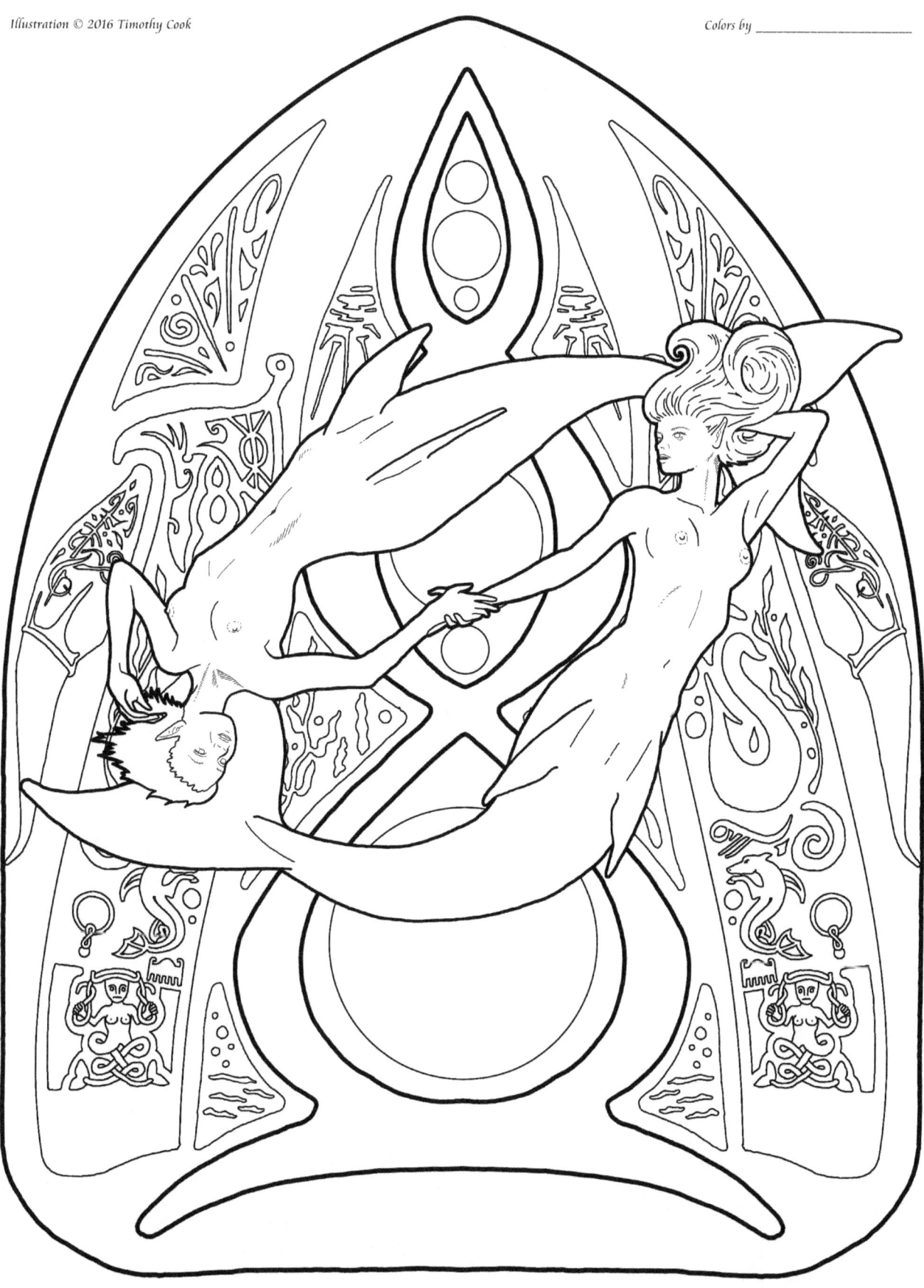

Colors by _____

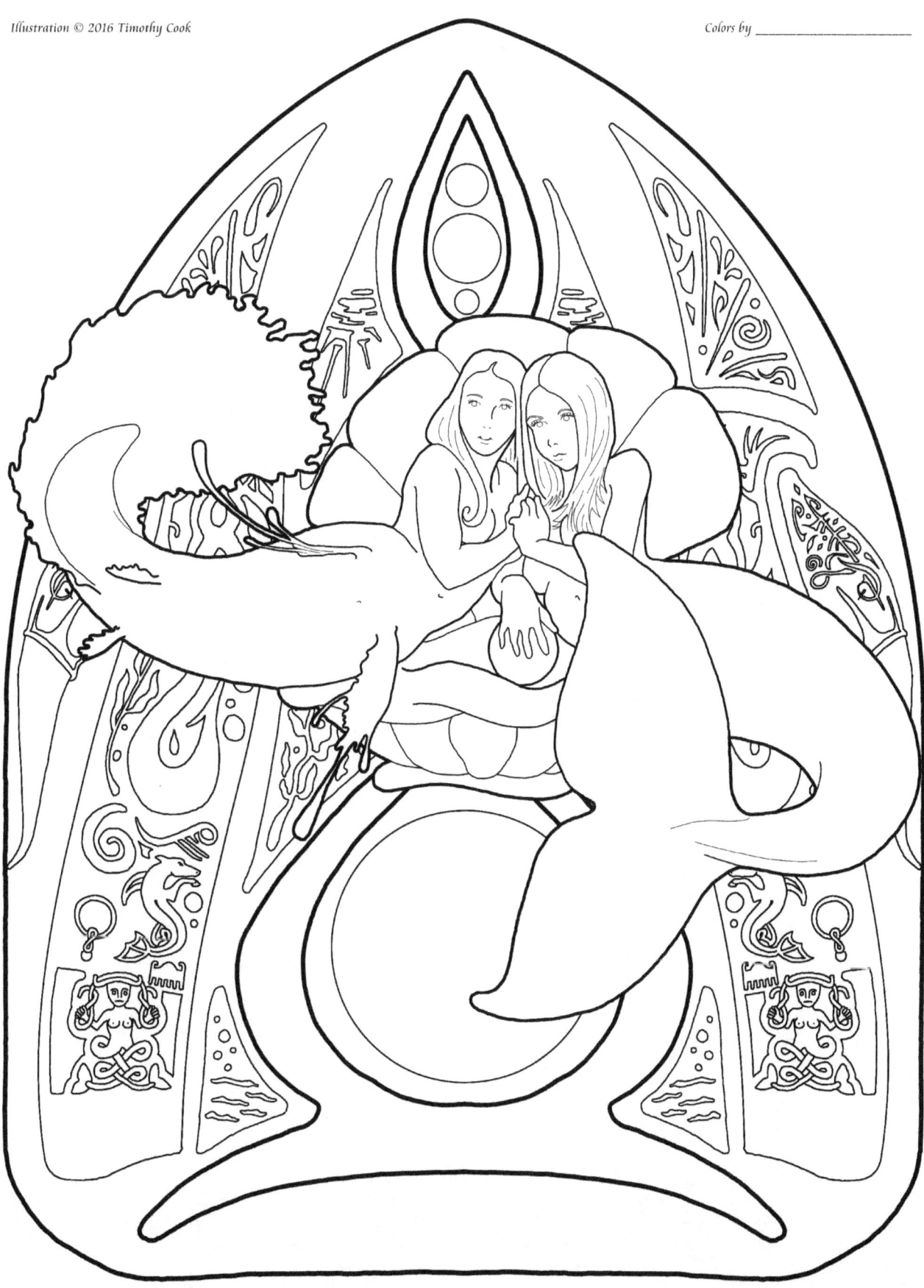

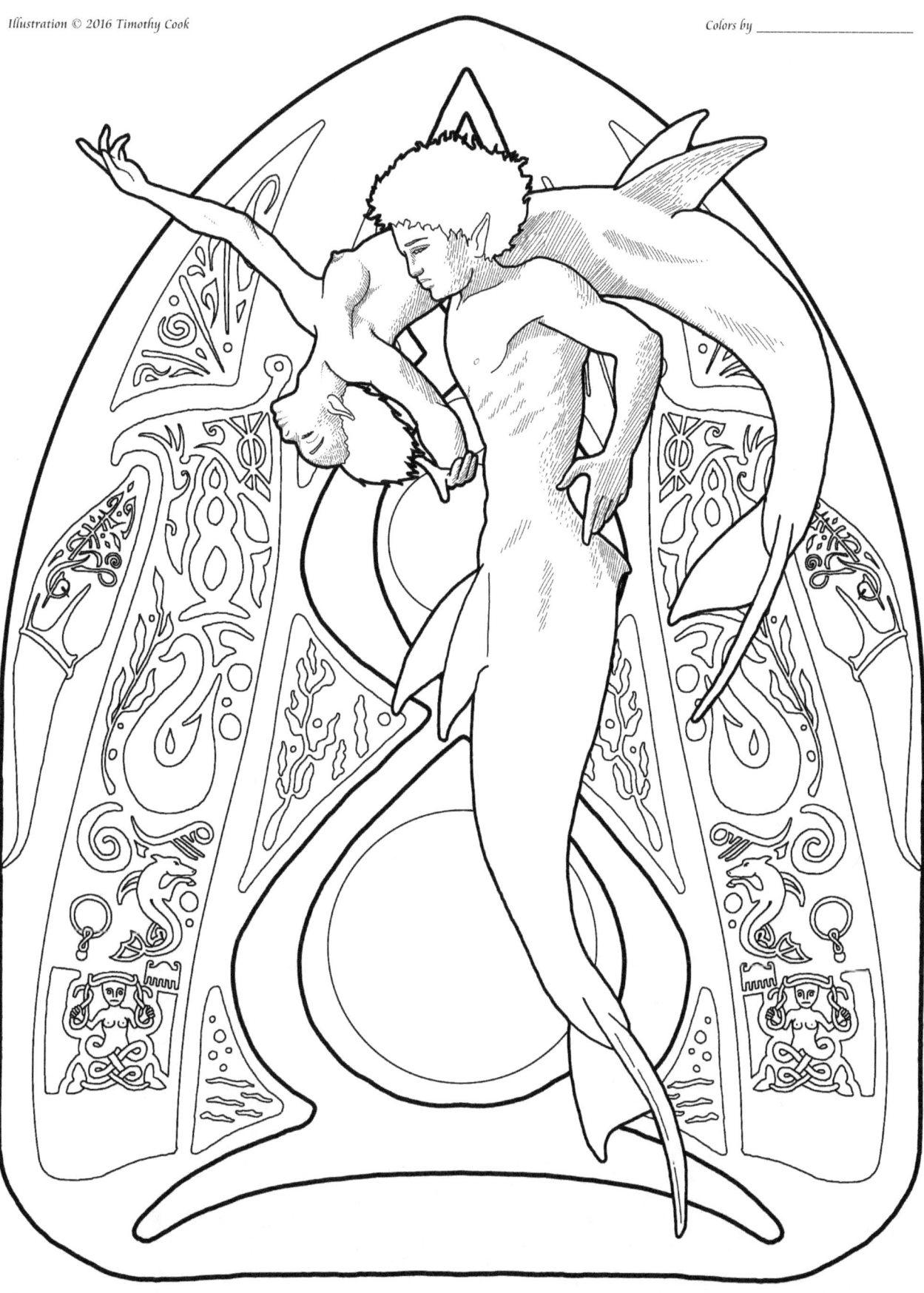

Colors by _____

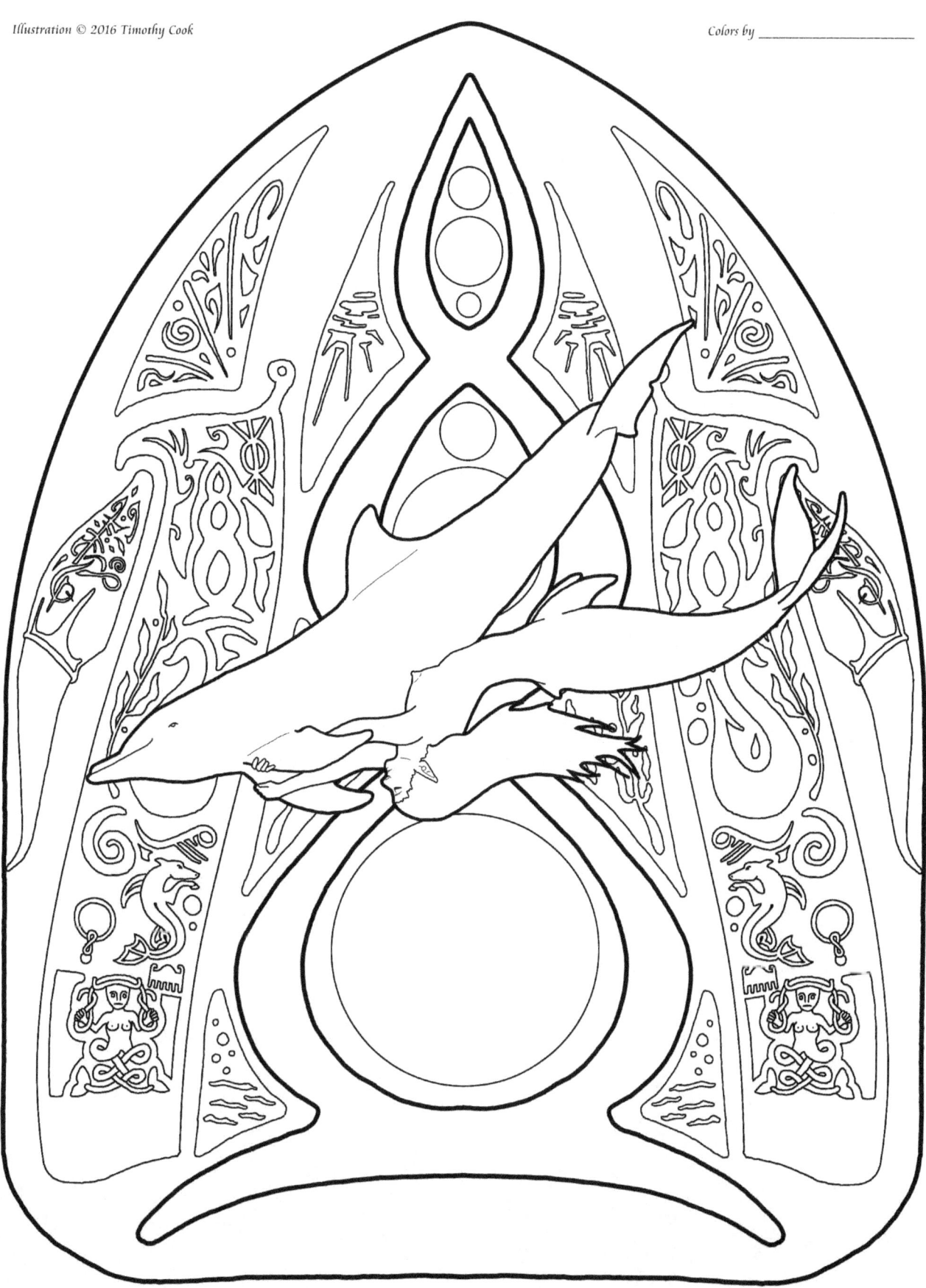

Colors by _____

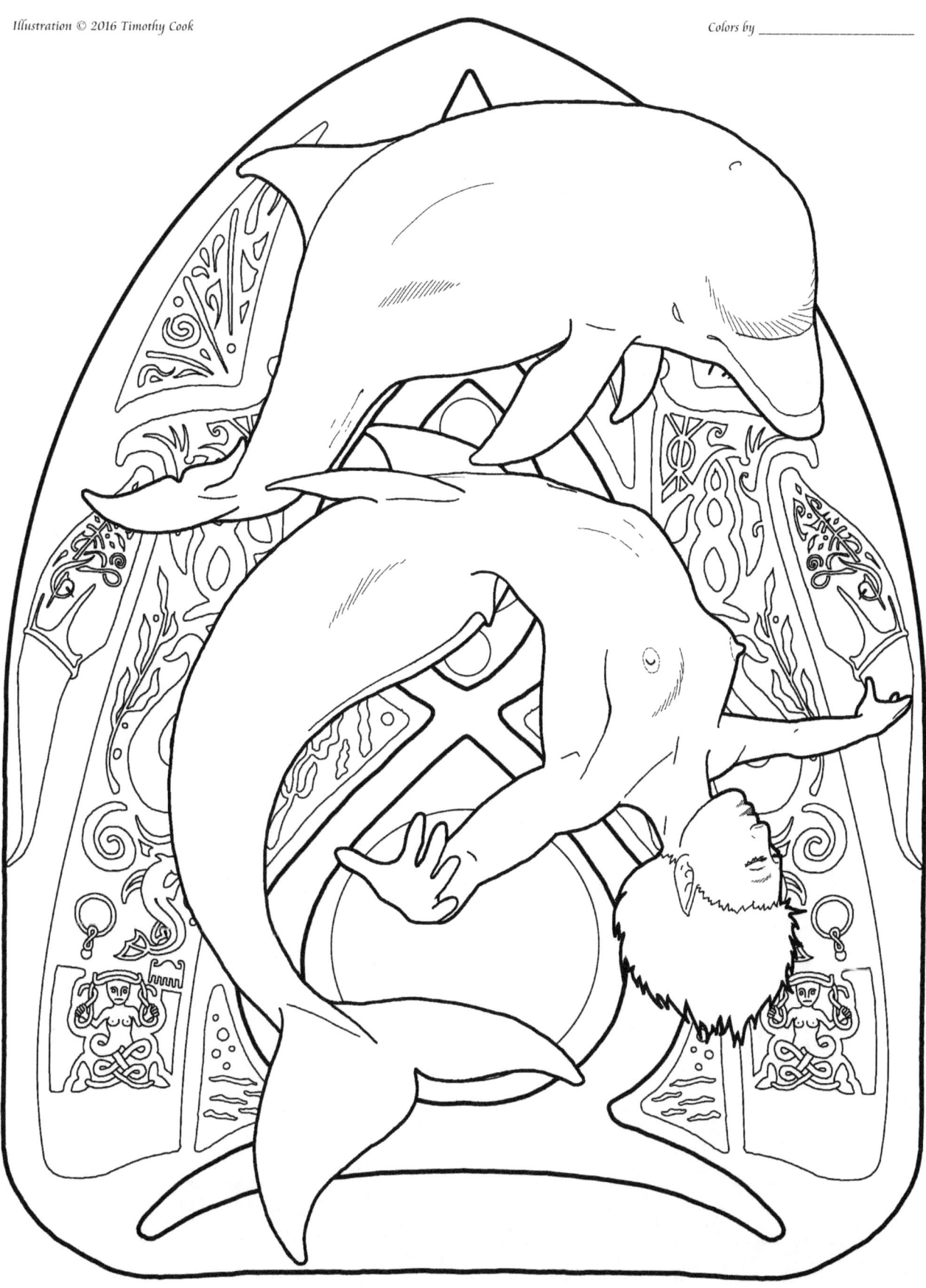

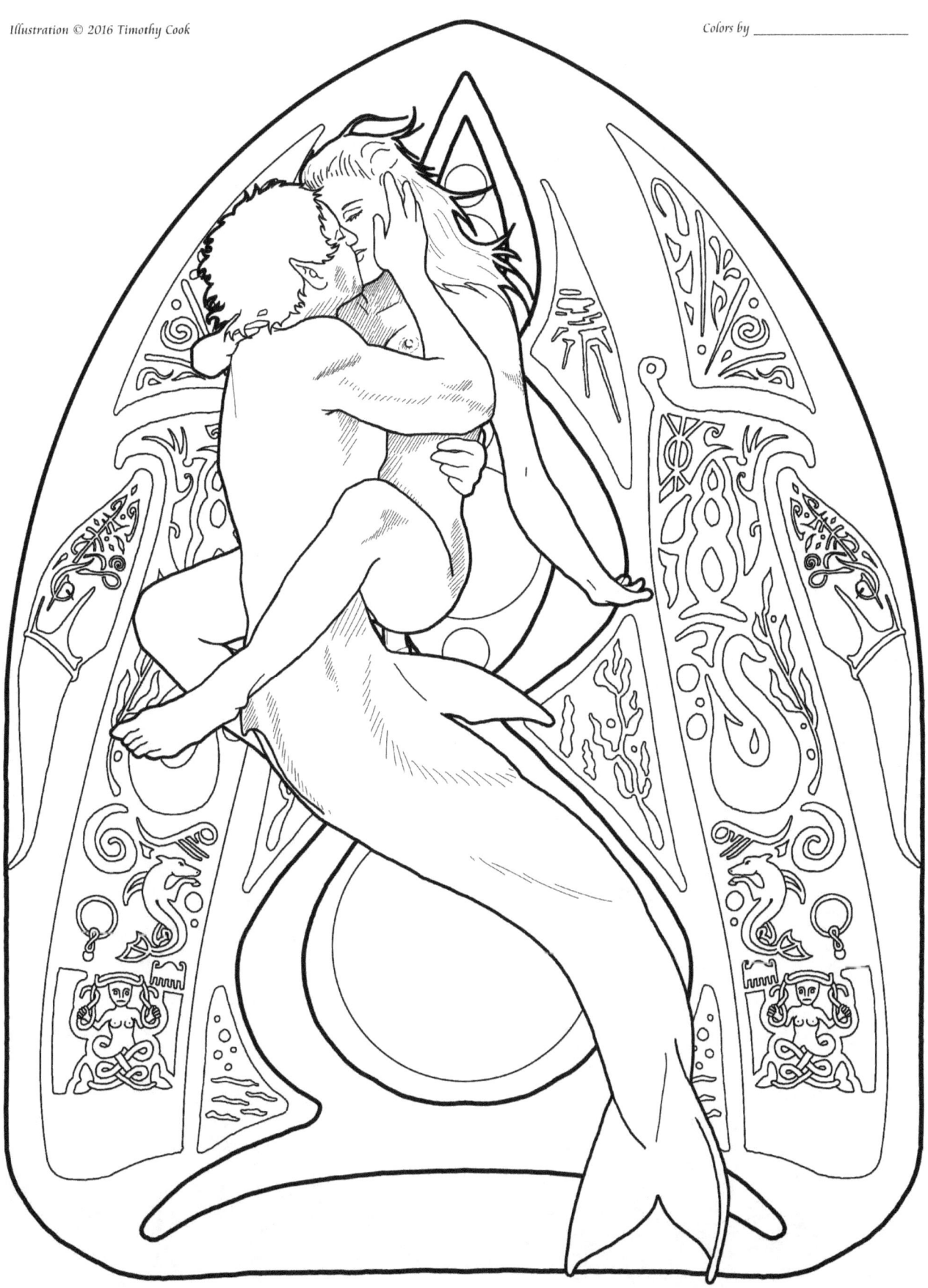

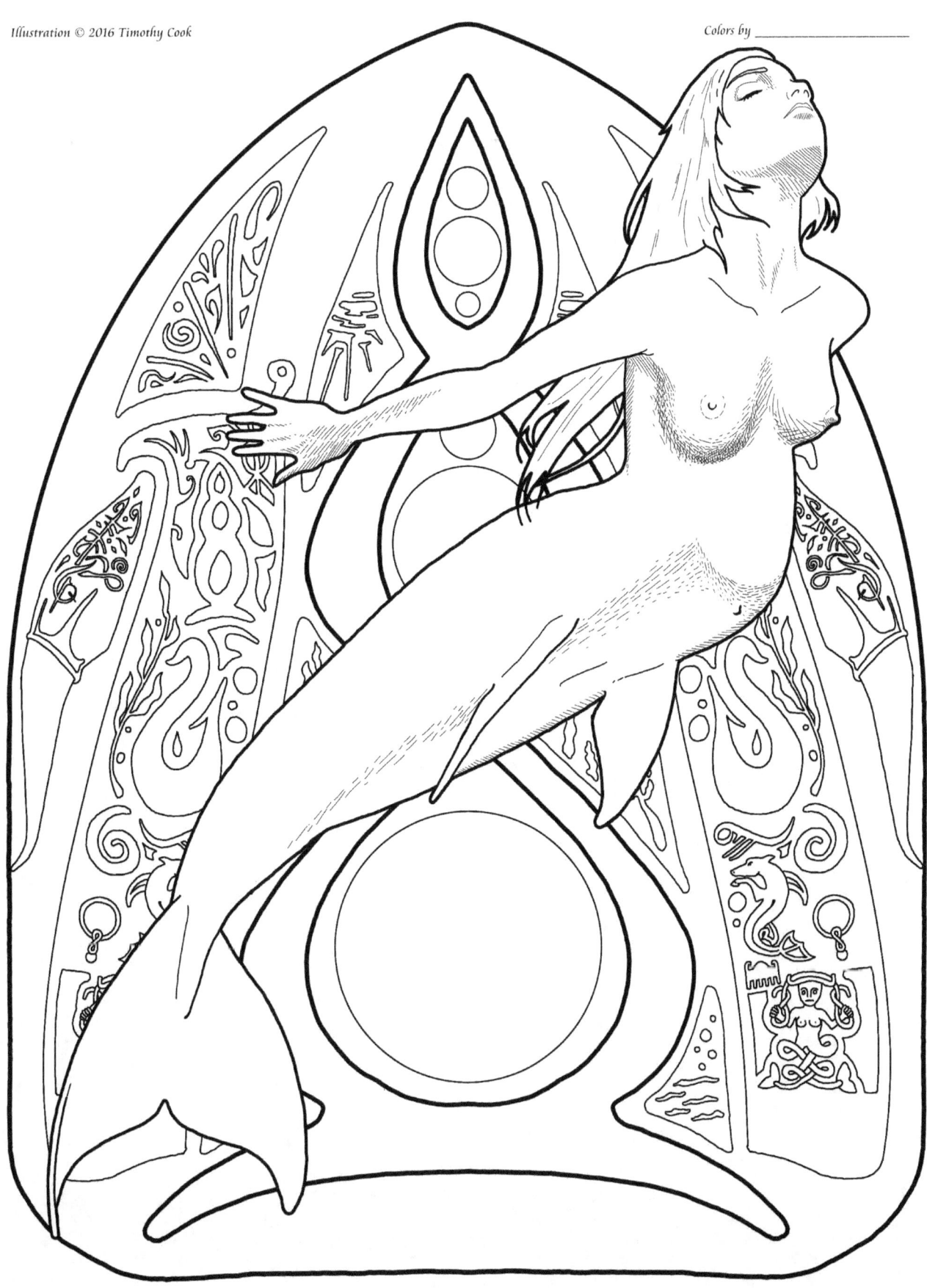

Colors by _____

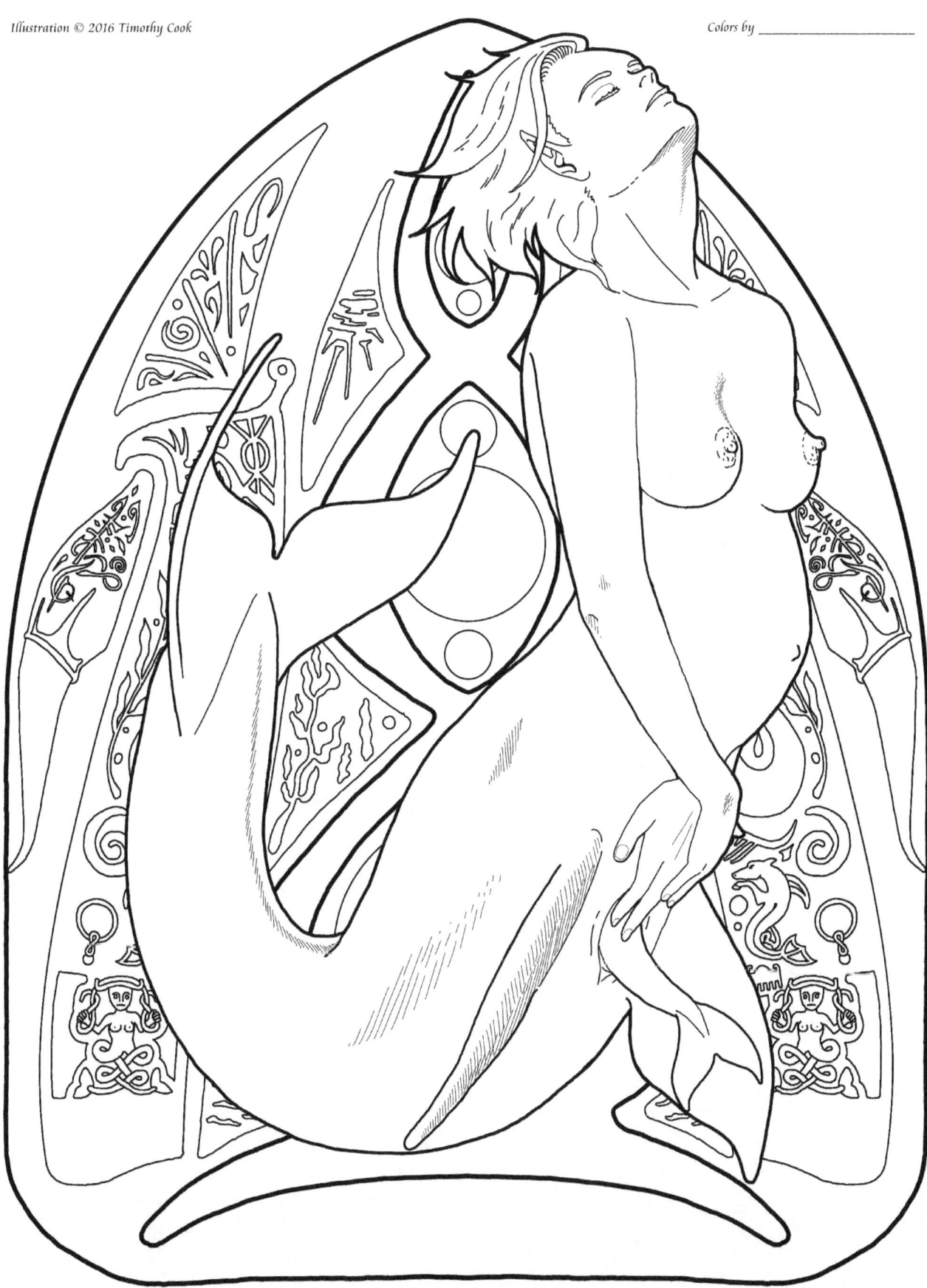

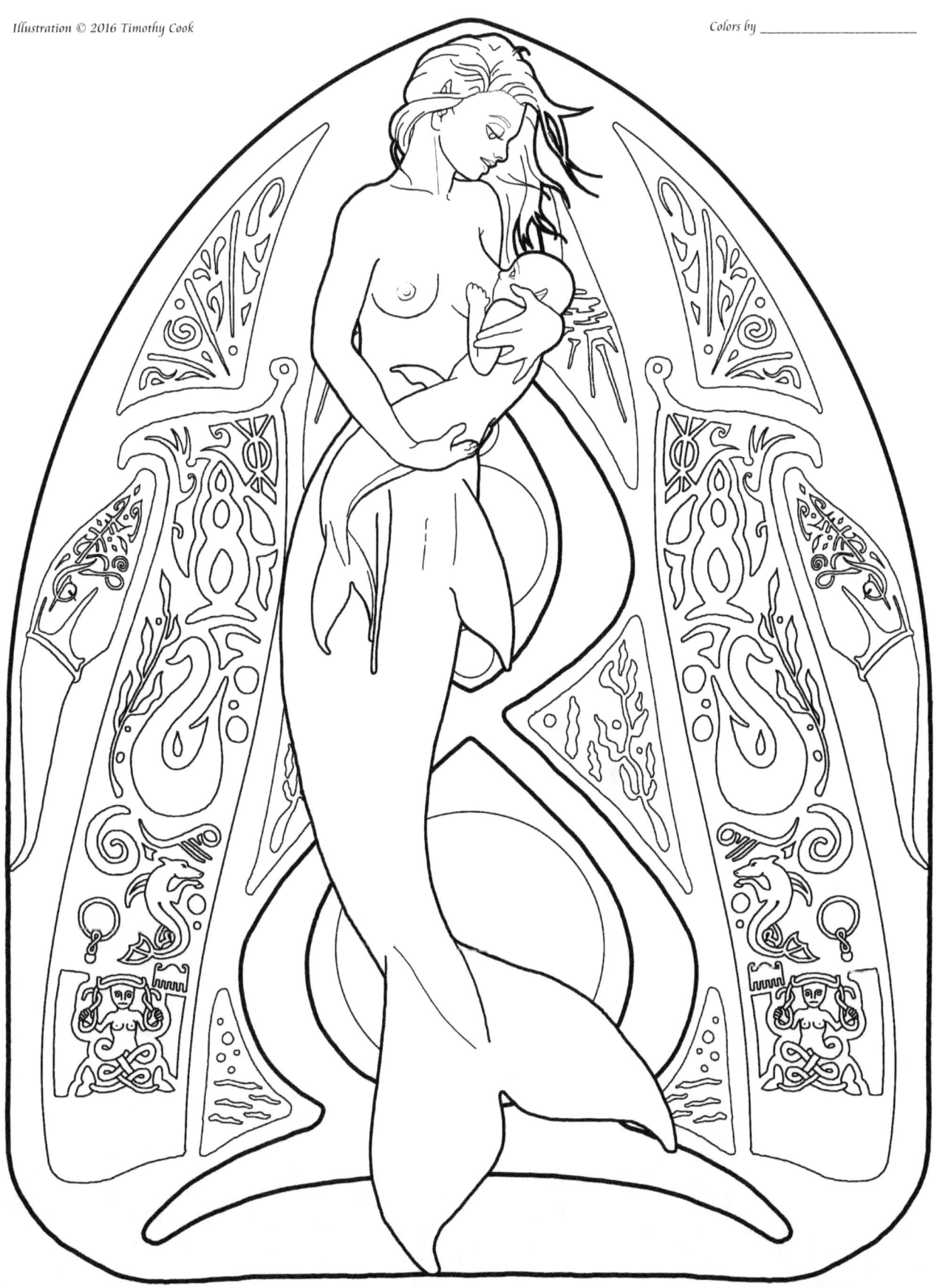

Part IV

couture

Attire worn by these mermaids elegantly flows in languid arcs, graceful lines and sheer fabric conveying a unified aesthetic that demonstrates unashamed acceptance of their bodies and trust of others.

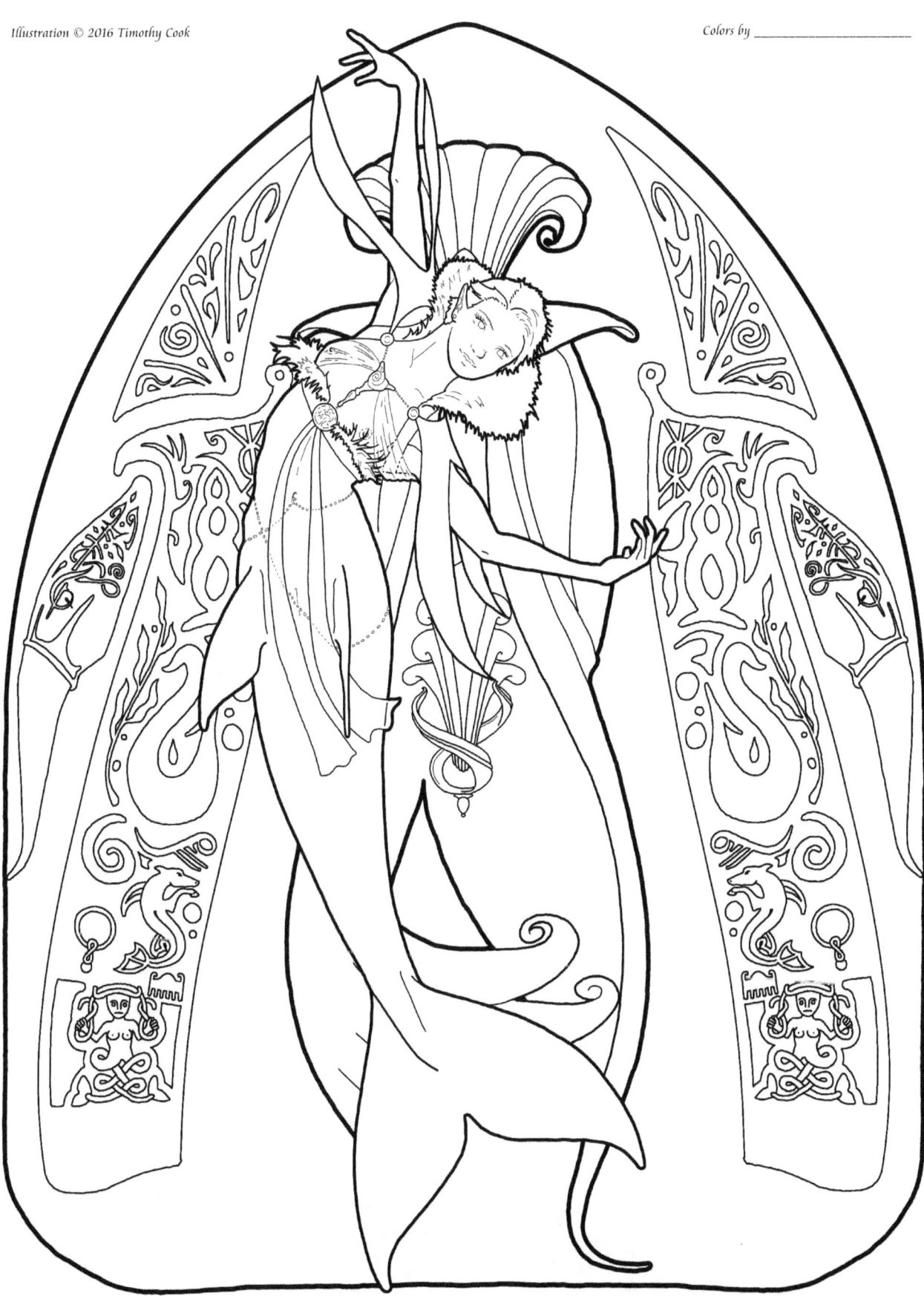

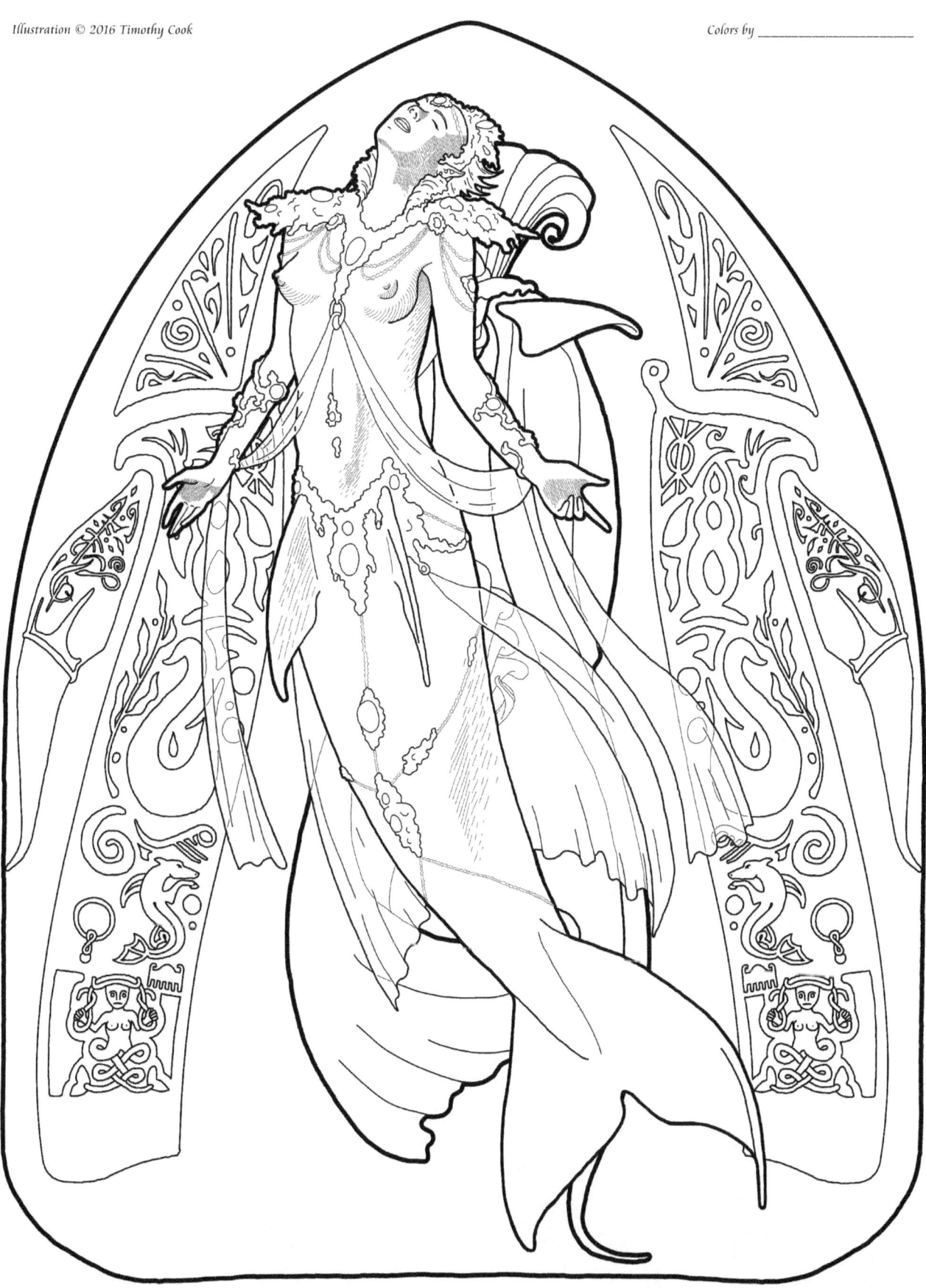

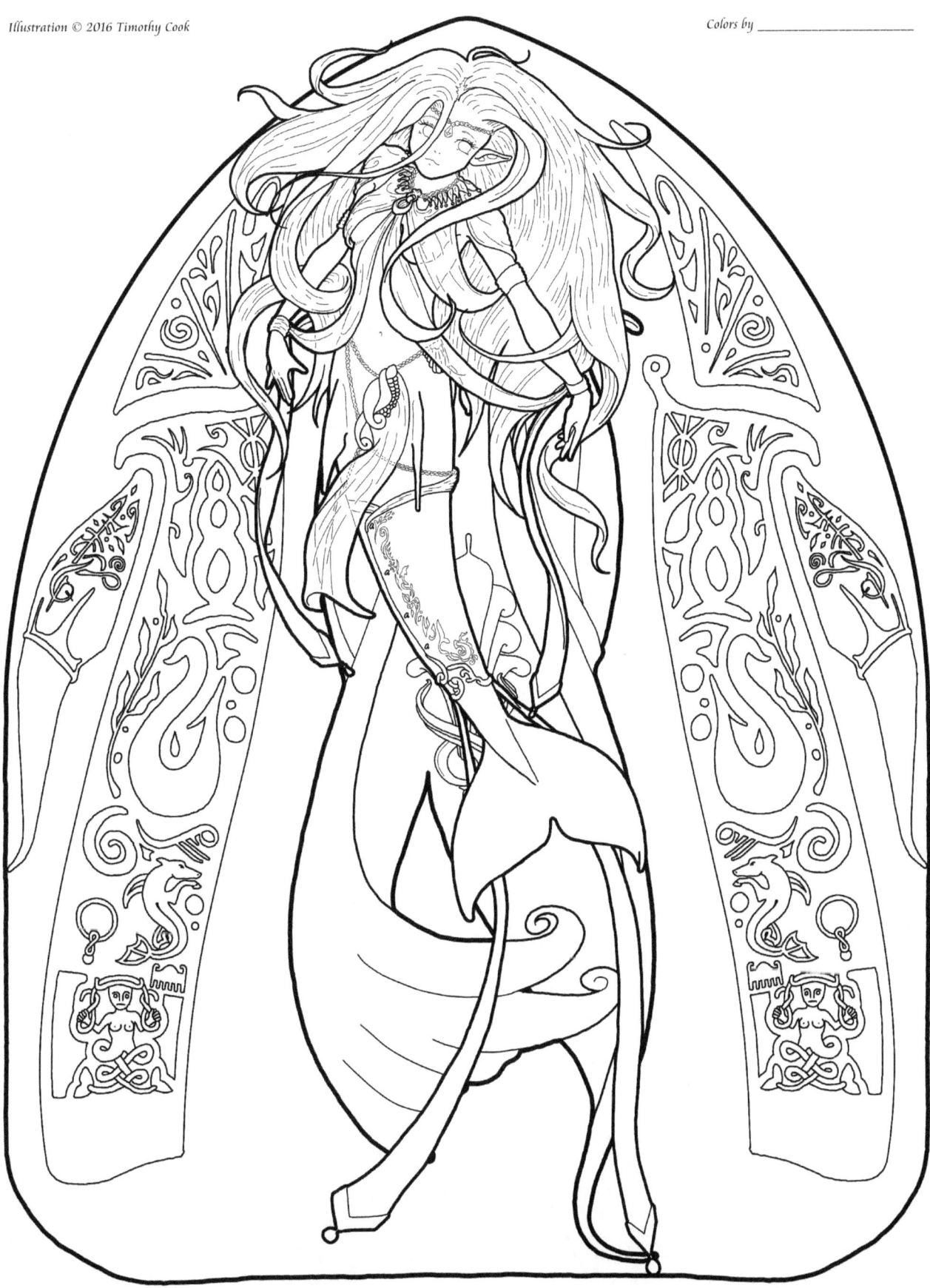

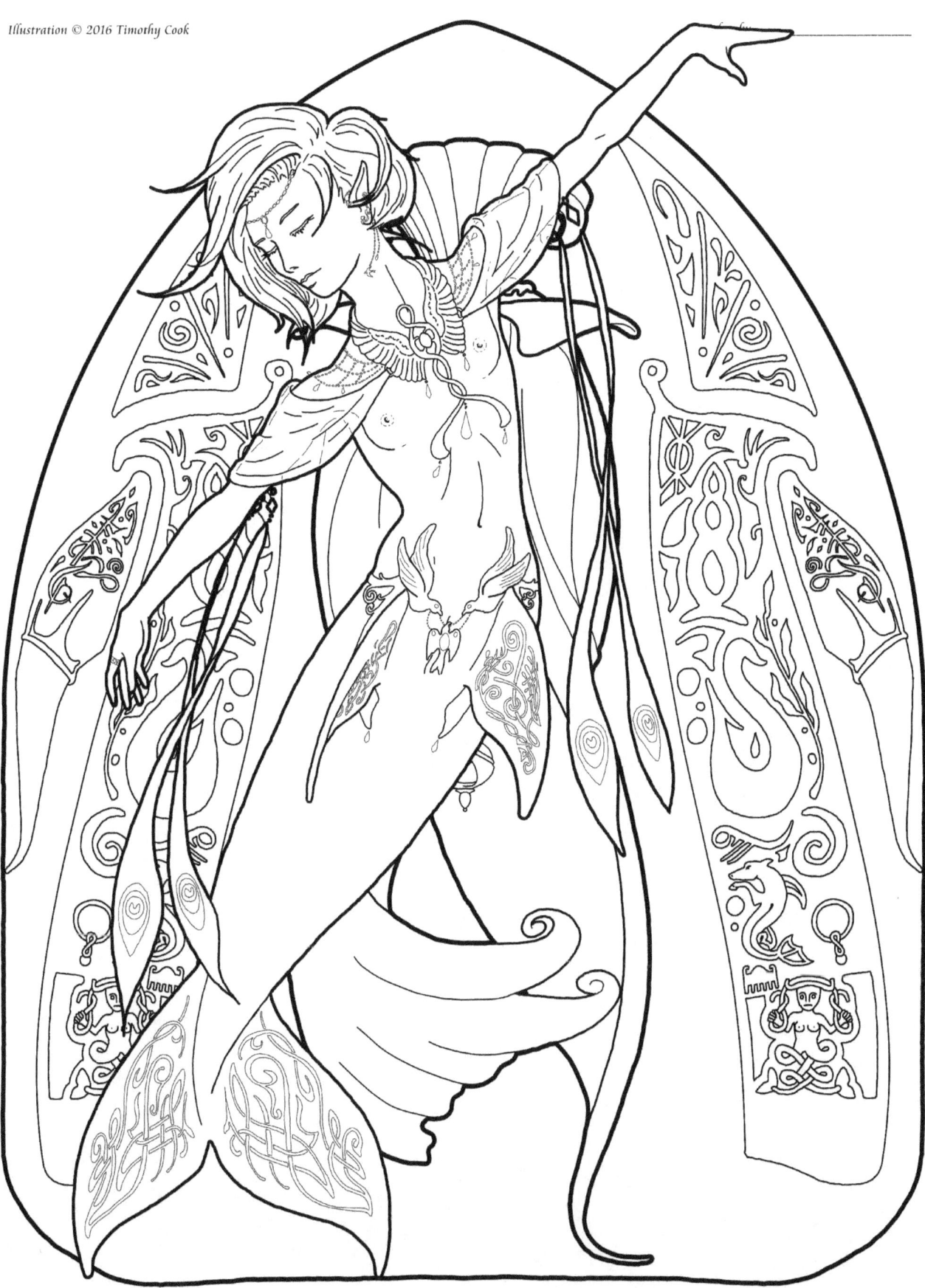

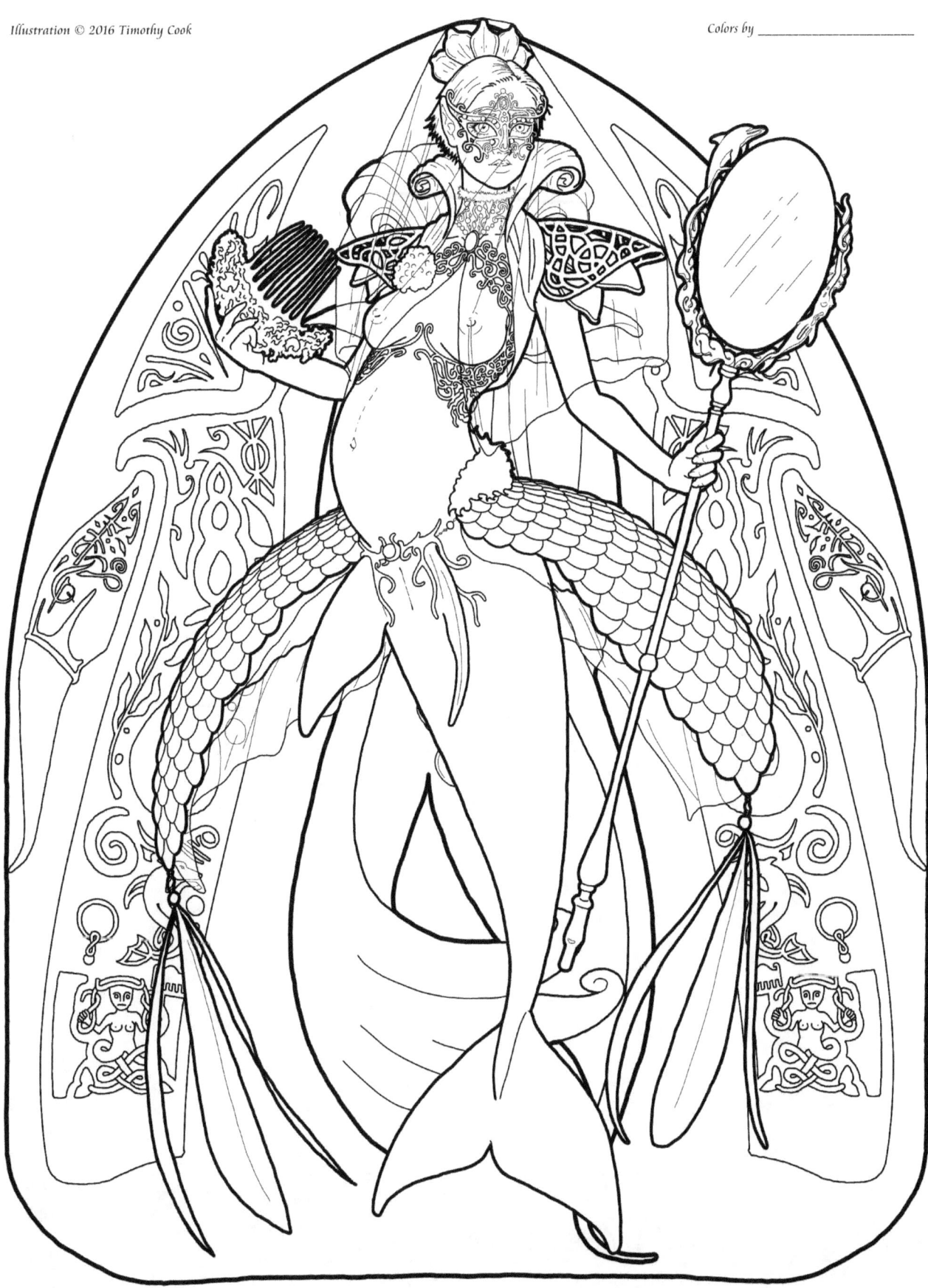

Colors by _____

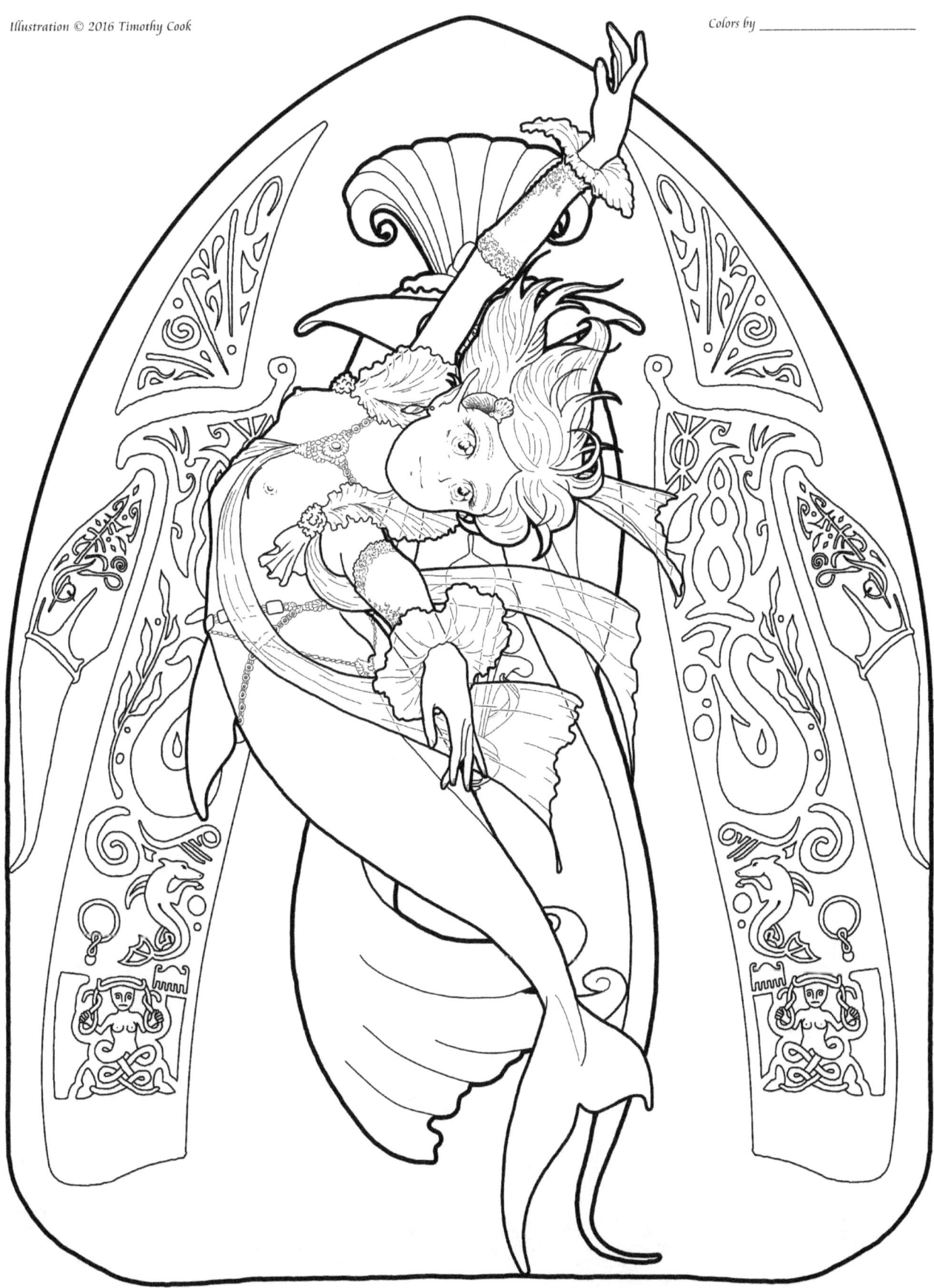

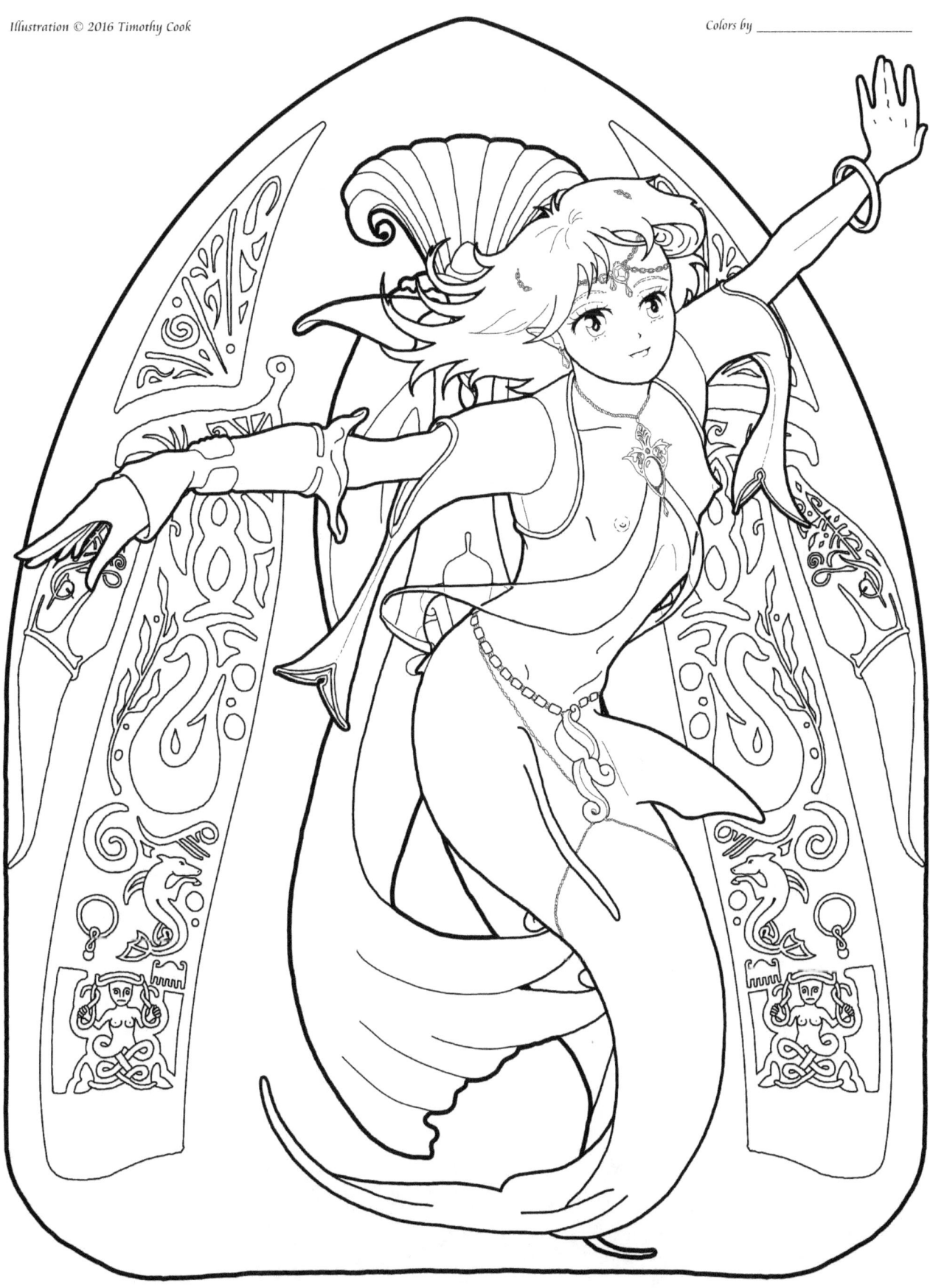

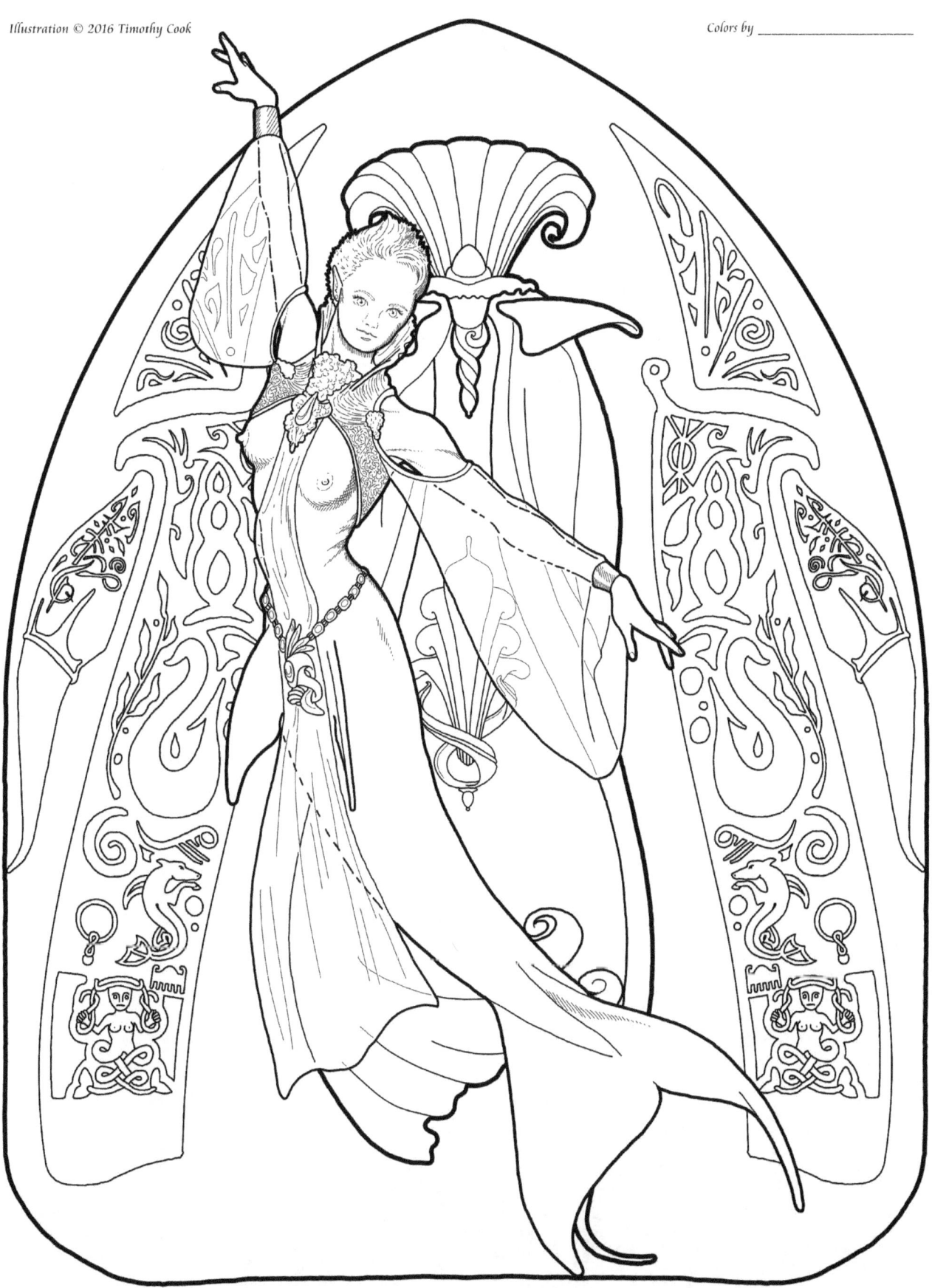

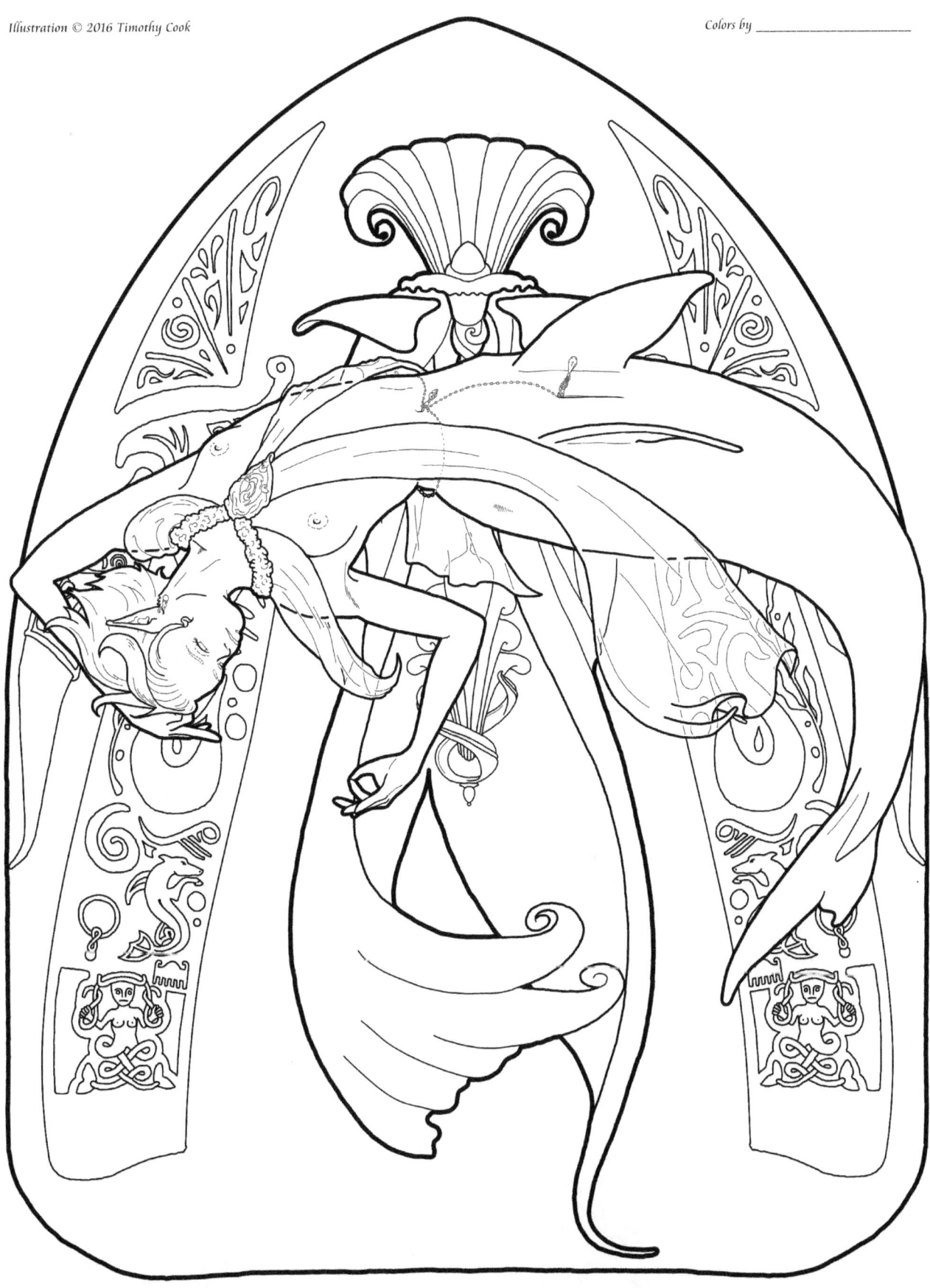

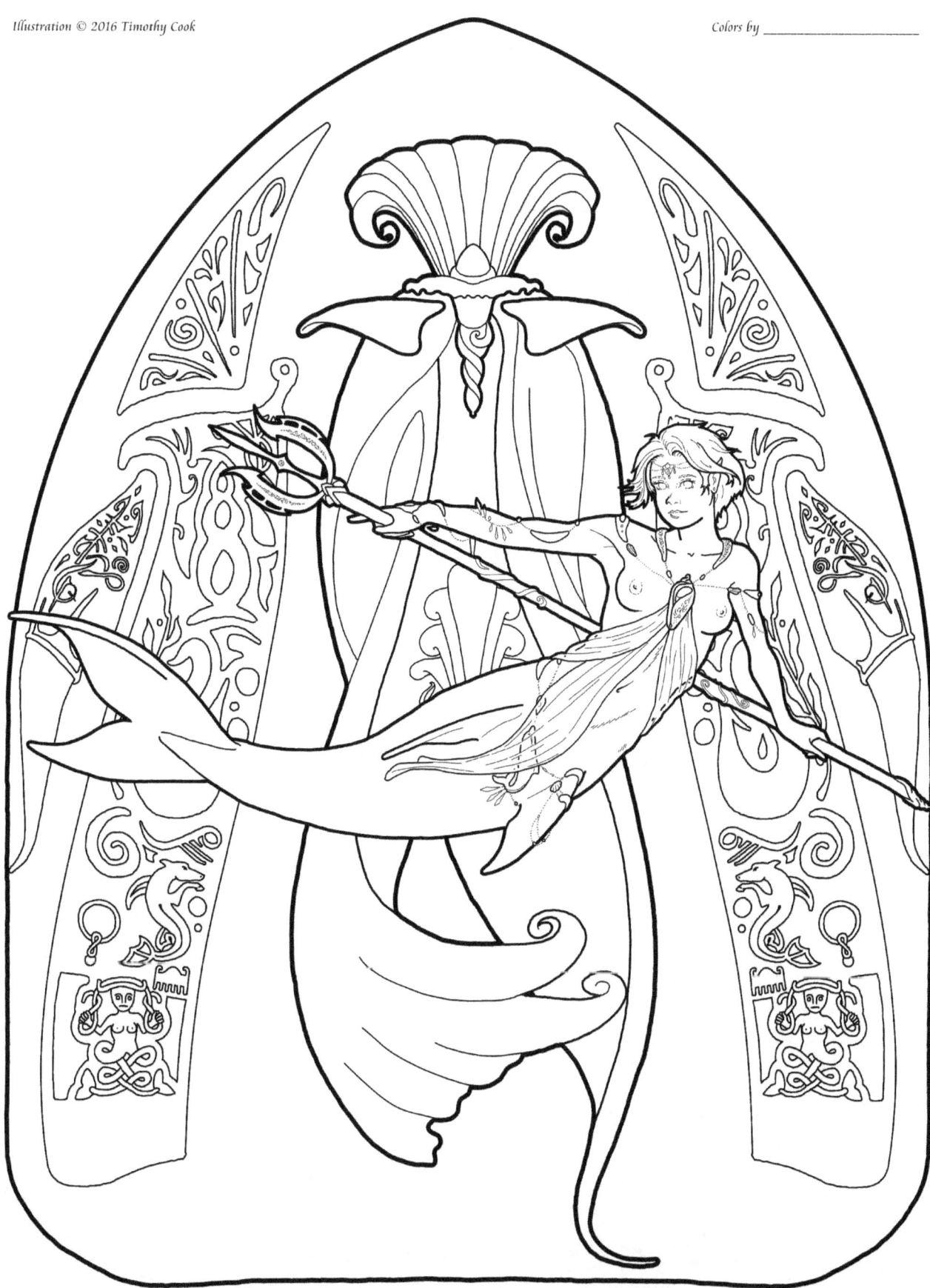

Colors by _____

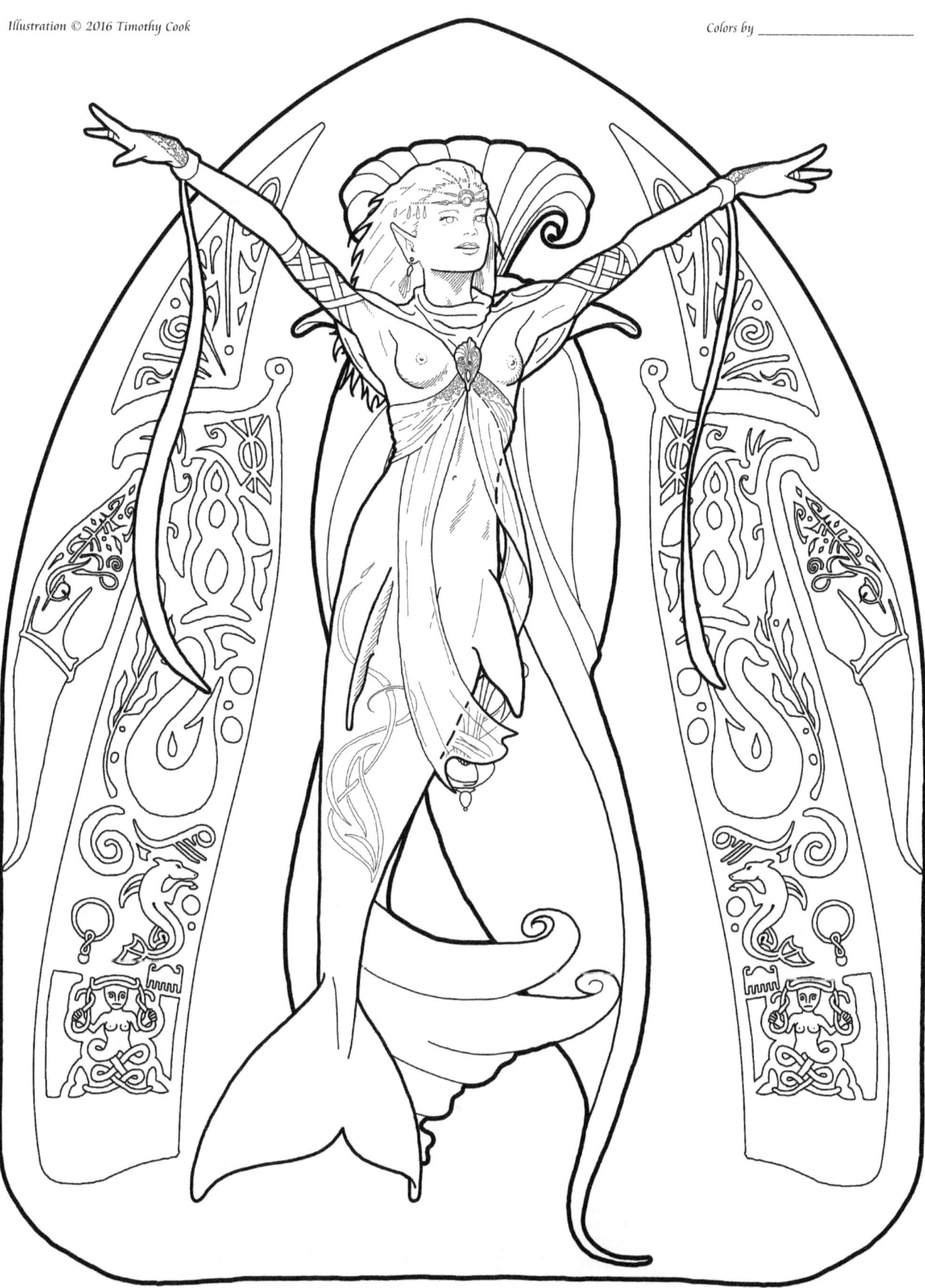

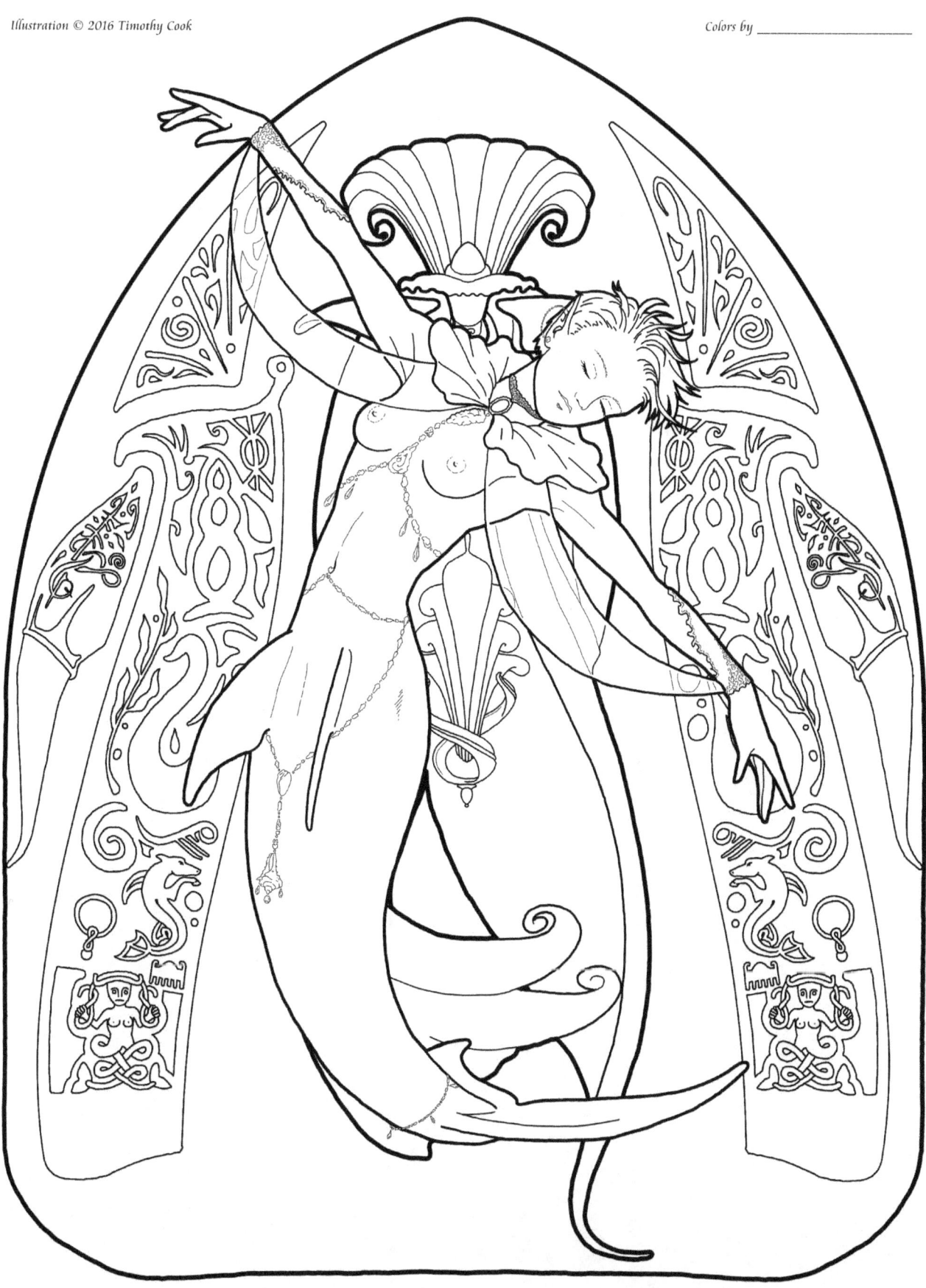